Diggers&Dreamers

The Guide to
Communal
Living
98/99

Edited by
Sarah Bunker
Chris Coates
Jonathan How
Lee Jones
William Morris

DIGGERS AND DREAMERS PUBLICATIONS

First published
1997
D&D Publications
BCM Edge
London
WC1N 3XX

ISBN
0 9514945 4 6
Paperback

Distribution
Edge of Time Ltd
BCM Edge
London
WC1N 3XX
(07000) 780536

Printing (contents)
Greenwood Recycled
Printing
Lakeside
off Warehouse Hill
Marsden
Huddersfield
HD7 6AE
(01484) 844841

Printing (cover)
Buckingham Colour Press
Riverside Works
Bridge Street
Buckingham
MK18 1EN
(01280) 824000

Typesetting and Layout
Jonathan How
BCM Visions
London
WC1N 3XX
(07000) 780910

Acknowledgements: Thank you to all our contributors and to the many communities, housing co-ops and other organisations that have responded to our requests for information. Once again we've been to several places for our meetings in the last two years, so grateful thanks to everyone at Bamford Quaker Community, Beech Hill, Old Hall and Redfield for being such generous hosts. When D&D 96/97 came out it was snapped up by Evelyn Marsden, one of our most avid readers and a great international commune-hopper. She wrote to us saying that she liked the book but, being a "pedantic old woman", was horrified by the number of typographical errors. She offered, there and then, to proofread D&D 98/99 for us. Sadly, Evelyn died just as the proofs were being prepared for this edition so we had to go ahead without her assistance. But we *have* tried extra hard to check for errors of all kinds and ... Evelyn, wherever you are, thanks for the offer. It was the thought that counted!

Contents

Preface

> *I think by the very fact that there are hundreds and thousands of people living in communes and are living a different way of life, they can make some people sit up and think "maybe there is another way of life, maybe we ought to change our way of life." Communes are not setting out to exert some sort of influence, they are not preaching – they have changed things for themselves and that is enough. If people want to follow, fair enough."*
>
> Founder member Shrubb Family,
> quoted by Andrew Rigby in **Communes in Britain**, 1974.

Welcome to the last Diggers & Dreamers before the Millennium. In this edition Colin Ward reviews the impact of a century of communal living on the landscape, we take a cycle trip to the Kibbutzim with Dave Darby and Sarah Bunker asks "Do we have to have magnolia walls?" We find out what Andrew Rigby got up to in the 60s, what Guinness got up to in Wandsworth and, as they say ... much much more. Hope you enjoy it. See you at the Millennium.

POST C

Sunday

Dear Jane,

God, what a headache! Went with Frank to that meeting last night — you know, the group that wants to buy the old pile down in Dorset or Devon or Dumfries (never was any good at geography!) and start a commune? No, hang on — we don't say "commune" any more, we say "community"! Much more millennium, Etzioni, Blair, all that stuff! Anyway, they had this red wine someone had made out of beebleberries, and we were all supposed to bond like some stupid rugby team and discover our group affinity for the great adventure! Save me from therapism! Some creep with wheat flakes in his beard had to hold my hands and tell me five important things about himself, and trust me — they weren't! Plus, Frank wasn't pleased! But we're all going to visit different communities over the next few months and pick their brains about achieving nirvana. Should be a laugh!

Love, Emily

Lost Sheep
An early lino-cut by Damien Hurst

Whiteway in the Landscape

COLIN WARD

Ancient squatter settlements, the 100 year old Whiteway Colony, the Plotlands of the early 20th century, and the communes of the 21st century, all share a common landscape. Colin Ward explores while on pages 16 and 17 Tessa Marin recalls her Whiteway childhood.

Historical geographers find recurring patterns of human settlement in the rural environment. They talk of "open" or "closed" villages and of "linear" or "poly-nuclear" forms of development. There is an eloquently nostalgic passage in **The Penguin Guide to the Landscape of England and Wales** that evokes the unofficial landscape. Its authors explain that

> "In order to sense the atmosphere of the pre-industrial rural scene it is desirable to leave the beaten track (as far as this is still possible) and seek out those corners of England and Wales where odd vestiges of that vanished era can be glimpsed. Such places are usually quiet and sheltered, devoid of features likely to attract the attention of the compilers of guidebooks, and unremarkable in terms of architecture, scenery or historical and literary associations ... The traveller may come across them quite unexpectedly, struck by an indefinable change in the scale and quality of the landscape ..."

One such category, they explain, comprises squatter settlements, those places that arose on the "wastes" on the edges and verges of parishes, and,

according to folklore were built between sundown
and sunrise, and whose occupiers scraped a living
on the margins of several occupations. As the his-
torians of the landscape put it, "The chaotic mor-
phology, with altered and patched-up cottages
(originally made of turf and branches) linked by narrow lanes twisting between the irregular enclo-
sures of the smallholding clearly reflects their
haphazard origin."

A twentieth-century variant of these secret places
was the kind of settlement for which town-plan-
ners coined the useful word "Plotlands". They
were the result of several factors. One was the
agricultural depression resulting from cheap food
imports that began in the 1870s and lasted until 1939,
with a short break in World War I.

This forced the sale of bankrupt farms at throw-away
prices, divided into small plots by speculators.
But it was linked with other factors: the spread of
the holiday habit and the idea of the "week-end",
the new cult of the open air as an alternative to
Victorian stuffiness, together with cheap rail travel and the safety bicycle. Until post World War II

**An aerial
view of
Whiteway
Colony near
Stroud.**

planning controls outlawed plotland development, unsellable agricultural land was divided into small plots and marketed, often in unorthodox ways, to people wanting to build their holiday home, country retreat, smallholding or rural commune.

The word evokes a landscape which, in its mature form, is very like the traditional squatter pattern. By 1939 it was to be found in pockets across the North Downs, along the Hampshire plain, and in the Thames Valley at riverside sites like Penton Hook, Marlow Bottom and Purley Park. It was interspersed among the established holiday resorts on the coasts of East and West Sussex at places like Shoreham Beach, Pett Level, Dungeness and Camber Sands, and famously, at Peacehaven. It crept up the East coast, from Sheppey in Kent to Lincolnshire, by way of Canvey Island and Jaywick Sands, and inland, it clustered across South Essex.

In 1984 Dennis Hardy and I wrote a long and detailed book about the plotlands of South-East England, **Arcadia for All**. It is long out of print, but we have hopes of a new paperback reprint due to the recent BBC television drama called *Plotlands*. But one thing we learned while writing it was that every other industrial conurbation in Britain once had these escape routes to the country, river or sea. For the West Midlands there was the Severn Valley or North Wales, for Liverpool and Manchester, places like the Wirral, for Glasgow the Ayrshire coast and even the banks of Loch Lomond, for the West Riding towns and cities, the Yorkshire coast and the Humber estuary, and for those of Tyneside and Teesside, the coasts of Northumberland and Durham.

It seems to me that we could almost describe a proportion of the population as obeying a law of nature in seeking out a place where they could build for themselves and do their own thing. But what is the connection between all these private dreams and the hopes of people with community aspirations?

There are several ways of looking at this question. The first is that the plotland settlers were obliged to develop a strong sense of community. This has been visible in the last few years in the case of a plotland site called Holt's Field in Swansea Bay. There the people who built their chalets in the 1930s leased the land and paid a nominal annual license fee to the landowners, the Holt family. But the new landowners are a property company seeing the site as having a development value of £2 to £3 million, and they sought to get rid of the 27 chalet owners. Swansea Council refused planning permission to the developer, declaring the site to be "arcadian" and designating it a Conservation Area in 1990. As I write, last-ditch appeals are being made to the House of Lords.

However, when Dennis Hardy and I were able to explore the plotlands of South-East England while plenty of the original settlers were still living, what struck us, just as it has struck people interviewing the residents of Holt's Field today, was their enormous attachment to their homes, their defensive independence and their strong community bonds. Frequently the sites that Dennis recorded in his book on **Alternative Communities in Nineteenth Century England** were in the same locations as those plotland sites that we subsequently described. The reason for this, of course, is that both were places where the price of land was very low, precisely because (and sadly for the ambitions of community settlers) its horticultural potential was small. The land where both communitarians or rugged individualists settled, was either too low and was subject to flooding, or too high and hilly, or had lost its fertility through unwise ploughing in the past.

The triumph of Whiteway in Gloucestershire, which is a hundred years old in 1998, is that it is something between a community and a plotland site, and has found the right mixture for survival. When she had lived there for 25 years, Joy Thacker felt impelled to gather its history from old neighbours and from the records. In 1993 she published – on her own – a really handsome book of 220 pages with 132 photographs of the Whiteway landscape, and I'm delighted to say that it is still available.

Whiteway's story was told by Colin Osman in the 92/93 edition of Diggers and Dreamers, and is well worth re-telling in the light of Joy Thacker's book.

The place was founded in 1898 when a bunch of Tolstoyan anarchists, mostly from Croydon, pooled their resources and for £450 bought forty acres of infertile ground and one cottage, to lead a self-sufficient simple life together. By 1920 when the Whiteway Modern School was started, they described themselves as, "People who, in an attempt to get away from the unhealthy influences of modern commercialism, have gone back to the land and thus escaped many of the stifling conventions which hinder the development of personality. These people hold their land on the principle of possession use only, and though living in separate bungalows, meet often for lectures, study, music and enjoyment of social life generally."

Even in those days, zealots were lamenting that ambitions to do without money and to hold everything in common had slipped out of sight and Joy Thacker, from a much later generation, remarks how "Some say that 'the electric' changed Whiteway, and it was

Whiteway Colony: The Social History of a Tolstoyan Community

by **Joy Thacker**

ISBN: 0 9521760 0 9
Joy Thacker, 1993
220pp hardback ● £13.99

(available from "Edge of Time Ltd" for £15.50 inc p&p, see page 224)

From its origins in the 1890s, Joy Thacker traces the history of Whiteway – the "Colony in the Cotswolds". A century after it, allegedly, failed Whiteway is still there. The events described in this book make clear how timeless the communal dream really is ... and also, indeed, the problems!

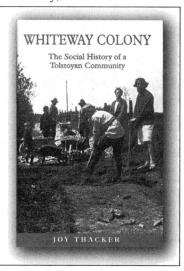

WHITEWAY COLONY
The Social History of a
Tolstoyan Community

JOY THACKER

never the same again," and she adds that "People visited a lot more then. Today the lanes are quiet. You may see someone walking, but it is more likely that they will be in a car, waving and mouthing to you as they rush by."

However, the great triumph of Whiteway, making it different from any other village in Britain, resulted from the first colonists' gesture right at the beginning. Having received the title deeds to the land, which they all signed, "they spiked the papers on a pitchfork, smeared them with paraffin and burnt them." The system arose that a person wishing to live there, or to buy an existing house there "must apply to the meeting for the land their prospective house stands on, and that on leaving it must be relinquished."

Working on the Dry Ground Road at Whiteway in 1924

In 1955 one resident claimed not to know of this convention and sought to sell her house and land. She took the case to the Land Tribunal in London, which ruled that "she had no title to the land; only to the building erected thereon." It also indicated

that the colonists as a whole were the licensees of
the land using a form of tenure dating from 1200
AD. *Freedom* magazine commented at the time
that,

> "The findings are interesting and enlightening, and
> however much it may have embarrassed some of
> the colonists to go to law, they are to be congratu-
> lated on the forthright and enthusiastic way they
> defended a worthy principle ... It is refreshing
> when courts are daily filled with people fighting
> each other over ownership of property, to read of a
> case in which people are standing up for the right
> of not owning it."

The author, in comparing Whiteway in its early days
with the mature, leafy settlement of today stress-
es that in some respects the rest of the world has
caught up with the colony. The pioneers stood
out because of their informal clothes, having dis-
pensed with "former incumbrances of corsets and
long skirts, stiff collars and boots", while all the men
wore their hair long. Today the rest of the world dress-
es like Whiteway residents. Similarly, dispensing
with marriage contracts is normal rather than
exceptional in the new generation, and the same thing
can almost be said of vegetarianism.

Her daughter, Vicky Thacker, contributes a valuable chapter on growing up in the mature Whiteway.
Attending the secondary school in Stroud, she
was aware of the rumours that used to be spread
about the nudist colony of mud hut dwellers, but
from her point of view, "Whiteway has always
been a comfortable place for children to grow up
in as everyone uses first names. A long tradition which
developed from the idea of complete equality
amongst the colonists. This meant that as a child
you were not cut off from the adults by formality."
And she adds that, "I do not think that children fully
realise the significance behind owning or not owning the land and it seems a shame that when they
do get to learn about the land-holding system, they
do not understand the principles and reasons
behind it."

The early landscape of Whiteway was raw and bleak. The pioneer settlers built moveable timber huts with corrugated iron roofs. "The ideal, from the early Whitewayans viewpoint, was where all possessions of the user-occupier would be cleared from his alloted land when he vacated it." Some did, but most accepted suitable payment from the incomer. But of course standards of housing have changed enormously. Water and electricity supplies came in the early 50s as in most other places in poor rural Britain, and some interesting pages are devoted to the ingenuity and hard labour the Colony applied to obtaining water, heat and light before those days. As anywhere else, a great deal of labour and expenditure has been devoted to restoring, rebuilding and extending houses. Joy Thacker raises the key issue that results:

"Therefore if the owner who has worked and spent time and resources on his home wished to leave the Colony, he expects and needs, if he is buying a property elsewhere, to get a reasonable return on his 'investment.' How else would he be able to afford another? The question we now consider is who, these days, can afford to pay outright for a large house, as opposed to the early years when newcomers bought small huts from settlers to enlarge for their own comfort? Will the time arrive when the only people who can come here are those with a substantial readily available lump sum? Who now, and in the future, will be in this enviable position? This sadly means that whereas Whiteway was a place where those of all denominations could aspire, as envisaged by Tolstoy, I am afraid that it will soon only be possible for those more fortunate who can afford it, but caring little about its origins.

"Alternatively, if you are content to remain on Whiteway, as most here are, then this situation has no significance whatsoever. For those occupants of colony land, however grand or humble their home might be, or whether their status in the eyes of the world is high or low, the common way in which we all hold our land is a marvellous unifier."

She argues that "the equality craved by those early socialist settlers has survived completely because of it, and will never change." I would add that the current position is not a criticism of Whiteway but of the situation that has evolved everywhere else. Capitalist land valuation and the constraints of our planning legislation have ensured that, a century later, nobody can set about a Whiteway or a network of Whiteways for the coming century.

But the good news is that a new, well-illustrated book tackles the issue of the landscape of communal settlements in a way that urges that the planning system should be positively encouraging a network of Whiteway.

This is Simon Fairlie's **Low Impact Develoment: Planning and People in a Sustainable Countryside**. If you know his name it is because of his involvement with the community known as Tinker's Bubble. He tells his own story in the introduction:

"When, with friends, I rented a house with a sizeable garden on a country estate, we were thrown out after three years to make way for a golf course. I lived in a van for two years, and eventually, with some other people, bought a bare-land smallholding. To accommodate ourselves we pitched tents on our land. In the

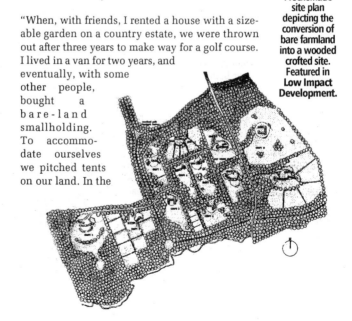

A schematic site plan depicting the conversion of bare farmland into a wooded crofted site. Featured in Low Impact Development.

Book Review

Chris Reid (a member of Redfield Community) reviews:
Low Impact Development:
Planning and People in a Sustainable Countryside
by **Simon Fairlie**

ISBN: 1 897766 25 4
Jon Carpenter Publishing, 1996 ● 162pp paperback ● £10
(available post free, from Low Impact, 20 St Michael's Road, Yeovil BA21)

Simon Fairlie's book **Low Impact Development** deals with, amongst other issues, ways of enabling development in rural areas that have a minimal or positive impact upon the country-side. Simon Fairlie writes from a perspective of someone who has direct experience of the planning system from the public side of the fence, having gone through all the possible stages in the planning application process, ranging from consultations, legal agreements, appeals, to a high court review as a result of his involvement with the Tinker's Bubble group in Somerset. This is a book that that considers rural planning in Britain from the perspective of those being planned for rather than from the professional planners point of view.

Fairlie's book is divided into two parts, the first documenting fifty years of rural planning, examining the effect that rural planning has had on the inhabitants of the countryside since the 1947 Town and Country Planning Act. Particular focus is on how the countryside has become "preserved in aspic", being now the domain of urban colonists who have no direct working relationship with it and how more and more people have become excluded from any possible way of making a living from the country-side.

The second part of the book, through the use of examples, acts as a guide to how low impact and environmentally friendly homes and workplaces can be built in the countryside without having a damaging effect. He makes proposals for changes to the law to facilitate such developments as well as how existing regulations could be used in a way to enable people to live on the land in a sustainable way.

This is a book for people who want to live on the land sustainably, and for planners who wish to make this possible it is also an important contribution to the debate on how society can develop sustainably in the future, both in the context of protecting nature but also being socially equitable.

two years since we moved onto our land, we have
been through almost the entire gamut of planning
procedure: committee decision, enforcement order,
stop notice, Article 4 application, Section 166
agreement, appeal, call in by the Secretary of State
and Statutory Review in the High Court. All this for
seven tents!"

And he goes on:

"If one is faced with eviction, on environmental
grounds, from a small tent on one's own smallholding, a stone's throw away from a new and
empty 30 foot high concrete block barn erected
with the blessing of the planning system, and from
a cottage occupied by a man who commutes to the
nearby town, one's initial reaction may, like mine,
be that the regulations are daft. However as one
learns how the rural planning system operates, one
appreciates that there is a logic in it; and that if that
logic is twisted, it is more by history than by the
planners."

Now since the British government is committed
to Agenda 21, agreed at the inter-governmental Earth
Summit in Rio in 1992, and since the phrase
"sustainable development" is frequently invoked
in the discussion of planning issues at both
national and local levels, Fairlie's exploration of
these concepts as an associate editor of *The
Ecologist* are immensely well-informed, as is his
great variety of case histories, and his fascinating
series of illustrations, ranging from the experience
of 'plotland' settlements to the Lightmoor project
in Shropshire or the work of the Walter Segal Self-
Build Trust. Yurt, tipi and bender-dwellers are discussed, as well as travelling people and the
Lowland Crofting policy adopted by West Lothian
District Council.

To me he makes a persuasive and unanswerable
case, all the more attractive because he isn't waiting for radical changes to the planning system,
believing that it is simply misapplied. He argues
that

Recollections of the 1930s at Whiteway by former resident Tessa Marin:

It was a muddly life being born at Whiteway! Our parents and other Whitewayans were building their homes, and all you could hear was the constant sound of sawing and hammering and an occasional "Damn!" because they weren't used to doing things like that.

I was born in October ... autumn was on us and Dad probably had the floorboards up – or rather not yet down! Later when they'd done all that they'd get us to slide up and down the floor with rags tied on to our feet to wear in the creosote. We did many errands, and had to get the drinking water from the icy cold spring; a pipe above the stream itself. We learnt a lot at the water-place: about siphoning, centrifugal force ... we made cups out of gypsy rhubarb leaves, looked at shrimps, crayfish and tiddlers ... and puzzled about the heartbeat of an enclosed ram pump. Life was always busy and interesting.

We used to torment our antagonists – mostly our parents – usually by chucking stones on their tin roofs, or in their water butts. At the same time the grown-ups were nearly all receptive, and had an open-door policy: we didn't ever have to knock, just open the door and call out. We called the grown-ups by their Christian names; there were only one or two that we called Auntie. We were always treated as equals, and we were very wild-and-free. There were colony ruptions sometimes, when of course we took sides as children do, but we grew up with very different values to those around in society, like thinking of others first. Trust was reinforced too, not taught, just imbibed.

But the things we liked the most were the communal activities, like working together on our limey-yellow lanes ... such fun. There were the long walks every month in the summer: a mile-long line of Whitewayans of all ages and sizes, and taking turns to choose the route. Then there was May Day – both a Pagan and international workers' holiday. Some of us were political from very early on. Although a community we were very aware of the outside world, and we had Spanish refugees in the Community Hall. Whiteway gave us as much explanation of things as we could have wanted, but there was not enough of doing things. We'd stand over people and watch them gardening, and building walls, roads and homes ... but they wouldn't put the tools in our hands. I couldn't learn like that – I had to do to learn.

There was so much ingenuity all around us, including in the arts: there was miming, plays, music, dance, a record club, films, puppets and shadow-shows. We were so lucky, and we knew it. Some of the older Whitewayans would shake their heads at us romping on the green... because they did have to work so hard, and spoilt us to a degree. We did like helping though: doing errands, fetching water, helping lift a crop, and we never expected nor accepted any rewards for anything. Indeed if offered anything, we were cross.

There was Ethel, however, who lived with Charlie in the spare house for emergencies, the one stone Cotswold one. She wouldn't go round to the shop, and always offered us sixpence to get her cigarettes – she made us feel we wouldn't be allowed to get them if we refused her tanner! Later Pat, a lovely giddy sort of Irishman, moved in with her and Charlie. He was one of my best friends, along with two other middle-aged men ... and younger kids, and older kids, and contemporary kids – we all mixed easily with everyone. We didn't compete much: everything was fair and natural, and since I did have an angry father to contend with, I suppose that made my life easier.

Rhoda, my Mum, ran a printing press with Dad's ingenuity to help, and there was always interesting paper about. I was tessa-marin-artist as soon as I could hold a pencil.

Our wooden houses were very cosy in the winter, hot and stuffy in the summer, when we were out anyway. I used to lie on the hearth making tiny, complete pixies and things for my doll's house.

Rose and Alf worked as a team in glass houses, and were always around. They were very important to us earlier, in the heady days of hot sun; they made a pool for us, and put sea salt in it. Rose was always firm and gentle with us, and read to us as well.

We'd dash about in thunderstorms and dip our heads into muddy puddles. We looked so funny.

When Brian (Smiker) tried to arrange cricket, we just socked the ball into Jennie's goosegog patch, and when he turned to football we all joined in: grannies including mine, kids all shapes and sizes, a few in unlikely shoes and skirts. It was like Alice's caucus dance in Wonderland.

We had plenty of creatures about; a tame duck followed me about and waited on door-steps for me. A bantam-cock rode around on my shoulder, wiping his beak in my hair!

We didn't eat meat, only a hen at Christmas, and we never had fried food except some bacon when we were on holiday camping.

Whiteway's in two pieces: the dry ground and the wet ground. We lived on the wet ground; as kids we kept to our patch, and didn't have much to do with the others until we went up the hill to go to dos.

One day planes were flying low over us; they'd just come up from Gloucester air-field. We ran in shouting: "air plane ... Mum ... AIR PLANE!" Everyone ran out and waved, and the pilots waved back! They had big gloves on, leather helmet and goggles. I saw an air balloon when I was about four; it was wonderful and I drew them all over my bedroom wall (I was allowed to).

Mum sent me to a private school in Stroud. It was a pity as I should have been with the others at Miserden, only a mile away. I was very adaptable, so it did me little harm being a bastard, and the only kid in the school who wouldn't join the Brownies. I wasn't going to do allegiance to god and the queen. I was the only kid in the school who didn't believe in god!

We heard about the famous people who thought encouragingly of Whiteway: some of the old Fabians, Gandhi, Dr Beneš, the Czech Prime Minister. I well remember sitting on Sylvia Pankhurst's knee! They used to come up for a rest from the fray.

We didn't ever know where babies come from, nor how they got started. The grown ups were discreet about their sex lives, and even more discreet about emptying the lavatory buckets.

I never took an exam in my life, and I'm proud of that. I was proud of my difference! Totally free of exams, I could think my own thoughts, built from what I learnt, and what I selected as **my** truth and understanding.

I've said and written lots about the lovely people who gave me time and knowledge. Daddy-Jim was one of my middle-aged friends: sensitive, frail, full of so much understanding of folks. There were quite a lot of interesting cranks, too, some with far-fetched diets, and others like my father who were escaping from conscription on the Continent, and used false names.

I remember we once scoffed at a woman who said, "I'm an anarchist – I can do what I like – I can go for a ride on the bus!" We said, "Aren't you glad the bus driver isn't an anarchist too?"

"If permission to build or live in the countryside were to be allocated, not just to those who can afford artificially inflated land prices, but to anyone who could demonstrate a willingness and an ability to contribute to a thriving local environment and economy, then a very different kind of rural society would emerge. Low impact development is a social contract, whereby people are given the opportunity to live in the country in return for providing environmental benefits. Planners will recognise this as a form of what they call 'planning gain'. The mechanisms to strike such a bargain are for the most part already written into the English planning system ..."

Fairlie's book seems important to me for people battling with the complexities of the planning system, because his aim has been to show that it could be made

"flexible enough to accommodate the radical new forms of development that the quest for sustainability demands; and to outline some of the ways in which local authorities can foster experiments in low impact rural development – some of them carried out at the margins of society, others designed to cater for more conventional people. These experiments – the failures and the successes – will be necessary to provide the groundwork which will enable planners, environmentalists and country dwellers of the next millennium to co-operate in the creation of a genuinely sustainable rural economy and environment."

His agenda is to encompass in the accepted environment all those unofficial landscapes; the hidden landscapes of ancient squatter settlements, of the Plotlands, and of century-old Whiteway, as well as of Tinker's Bubble and the five-month occupation of the derelict Guinness site at Wandsworth by the campaigners of The Land is Ours. There is a thread of communal aspirations that links them all.

In addition to **Whiteway** and **Low Impact Development** the books mentioned by Colin Ward are:

Arcadia for All: The Legacy of a Makeshift Landscape by **Dennis Hardy & Colin Ward** (London: Mansell 1984. Out-of-print, but a reprint is expected)

Alternative Communities in Nineteenth Century England by **Dennis Hardy** (London: Longman 1979. Out-of-print, but your library will have it)

Colin Ward is an anarchist writer. Many of his books are about popular and unofficial environments and are available from Freedom Bookshop, 84b Whitechapel High Street, London E1 7QX. His latest book is **Reflected in Water: A crisis of social responsibility** (London, Cassell 1997).

POST CA

Wednesday, Dear Jane,
Ok, I know I'm as middle class as they come — I don't deny it!
— and one of the reasons why Frank and I are checking out
this idea of communities is so we can broaden our thinking, and
move away from materialist values and get some fresh air and
yes, I'll even grow organic turnips if I have to, though I certainly
won't eat them! But I still think there are minimum, basic,
rock-bottom standards that it's reasonable to expect, even at
communities like the one we went to last weekend (Somerset,
I suspect) where they've been building the house brick-by-brick
for the past five years, all of them on the dole, though now of
course they're all Job-Seekers and they're being threatened
with re-training as sheep-shearers or Web page designers.
Anyway we get there Friday night and there's no electricity
so we get shown to the Visitors' Room by candle and we fall
into bed and it's freezing (but they're all like that) and then
around midnight I feel something wet in my ear and I go to push
Frank off but he feels all woolly, and I scream and there's a
sheep grazing by the side of the bed because (we discover at
daybreak) there's no floor and only three walls! Rustic, or
what!? I think I've got pneumonia ....
Love, Emily

Cybershear – The Sheep Shearers' Web Site
http://www.furryfleece.co.uk

From Genius to Genesis

NICOLA GRAYDON

Four hundred people, low-impact homes, vegetable gardens,

sunflower beds and surreal sculptures turned thirteen acres of

derelict land into a very unusual kind of community.

In 1996 a bunch of land groupies rescued a lacklustre London summer from monotony by invading a piece of wasteland in Wandsworth and turning it into a bizarre oasis. The oasis – called Pure Genius, to tweak the tail of Guinness, absentee lords of the land – became a living legend among eco-activists even as the geodesic dome rose out of the dust on the day of the invasion on May Bank Holiday.

The occupation was an audacious media stunt by The Land Is Ours – a radical landrights movement – to highlight the waste of urban land left derelict by developers and big business. Protesters planned to occupy the riverside site for a week, build a sustainable 'eco-village' with gardens and low impact housing, work with the local community, call a halt to Guinness's plans for a superstore and seduce a cynical press. In the end they stayed six months and exceeded expectations.

The place was a mess, but it had potential. It was littered with concrete rubble, wire and broken pipes but Nature had been at work during the seven years of dereliction. Buddleia bushes shaded nesting birds; saplings of Norway maple, sycamore and horse-chestnut were growing in the debris;

mugwort, hemlock, willowherb and buttercups had taken root and tall plane trees sheltered it from the main road.

Only three people knew the location, such was the secrecy surrounding the invasion. The rest of the 400 or so activists travelling on hired coaches to claim the land thought they were going to an industrial site in Croydon. By comparison this was paradise. "It's great," said Green Dave, one of the first to arrive and last to leave. And it was. A great, green space with fantastic views over the Thames.

Throughout the summer, a community flowered along with marrows, beans, sunflowers and other crops. It began to look like a massive adventure playground with Tolkienesque houses, surreal sculptures and winding paths painted rainbow colours. And it provided all the things a good oasis should: shelter, food, company, feasts and fights.

For me, and other wayfarers who drifted in and out of the settlement, it was a relief from the urban blitz and a glimpse at a different way of life built with the things that London throws away.

In many ways, the occupation marked a turning point in the direct action movement of this country. Combining protest with a constructive alternative, it drew a diverse group of people. Hard-core activists worked with engineers, architects, permaculturalists, planning experts and conservationists. People with wildly different expectations and experiences found common cause in pushing the dream to a solid reality.

There was little in the way of conventional organisation. The eco-

Jules face paints a youngster inside her house.
Photo: Brian Warrinor

residents met regularly in the Round House, with its wood burning stove and removable walls for summer sun, windmill, telephone and rusty typewriter. Mostly the meetings stretched debate beyond patience, taking consensus politics into anarchy, but they were saved by the purpose of a core group who chose to make this scrubland their home.

Green Dave took about a week, discounting time lost to weather and lack of materials, to build his house. Based on Scandinavian design, it was raised from the ground to prevent damp and boasted a conservatory to trap sunlight. He was a familiar sight wandering naked around the site holding a hammer and muttering to himself.

Anya, a disillusioned architect, built a yurt, the semi-permanent structures favoured by Mongolian nomads, and a prerequisite for land protesters. It was spacious, with light streaming through hazel lattices.

Kids gathered at Jules and Brendan's place where a double bed lay on stilts above a room built for tea and cider, ideas and gossip. Their place felt as though it could withstand a thousand winters.

The beginnings of Round House – made entirely out of salvaged wood and hard work.

Photo: Nick Cobbing

For a moment it seemed a perfect illustration of true anarchy in action: the belief that human beings are naturally benevolent and, with co-operation and freedom can live justly and harmoniously without governmental institutions. This was so benevolent, I forgot that I had wondered if I had the right to be there.

For a moment it seemed a perfect illustration of true anarchy in action

But, of course, it was not perfect and cracks began to show long before the bailiffs arrived. There were many reasons why: the flux of a constantly moving population meant that the burden of continuity fell to too few; too many people took advantage and drained the oasis dry and, finally, Pure Genius fell victim to its own success. Social services and homeless agencies sent their refugees to the site and drugs and violence brought fragmentation as the collective tried to reach consensus on what should be done. Eventually the original settlers and other committed change-merchants retreated to their homes. The Round House was left to the Brew Crew.

But Guinness must take most of the blame for the death of the dream. The constant stress of an impending eviction made it impossible to build a future. The protesters fought a sophisticated campaign to persuade them to use the site as an avant-garde tool for their environmental and PR department, but the multinational dug their heels in.

It was profoundly disappointing that a company which sells itself on the back of a funky advertising campaign, greenish policy and a family who pioneered low cost homes, failed to notice the potential of a sustainable, low impact, eco-friendly housing estate. Instead 200 police, bailiffs and security guards were moved in to evict the site, bulldozers crushed homes and industrial saws felled the mature trees which lined the site.

The night before the eviction was a long one. Dispirited by the impending loss of their homes, fighting talk turned to despair as the residents prepared themselves for the inevitable. Chaos crept closer as anger turned in on itself. Someone set fire to the healing bender. A chain reaction of bonfires followed, Jules and Brendan drenched paper in lighter fuel to help their home burn – but they couldn't do it. Green Dave chained himself to his bed. George Monbiot, one of the guiding forces behind the occupation, and six others from The Land Is Ours barricaded themselves into Bill The Builder's wooden Tardis. The rest climbed onto the Round House roof or locked onto the jetty which still proclaimed LAND AND FREEDOM.

Brendan paints the sign for the Wandsworth Eco Village.

Photo:
Brian Warrinor

The stormtroopers who streamed on site in full riot gear at dawn must have felt faintly ridiculous to be met with so little resistance. The police spokespeople told the press waiting at the gate that the site was a health and safety hazard, "with syringes and cess pits where the protesters had been defecating."

It was a malicious eviction. Organised the day before the site was to be designated a Site of Metropolitan Importance by the London Wildlife Trust. Guinness' hired help destroyed even the tenacious buddleia bushes and saplings. Now, writing in the Spring of 1997, almost a year since the May Day invasion, Guinness is trying to sell the site which looks like a cross between a car park and a concentration camp. They must surely regret their lack of vision.

Meanwhile the progeny of Pure Genuis have taken root: local Wandsworth residents, empowered by the village, have set up the Gargoyle Wharf Community Action Group to draw up plans for the site and lobby whoever is brave enough to buy it. Pure Genesis – formed by the long-term occupiers of the site – is organising more direct action and a boycott of Guinness.

Shards of energy were transplanted to Fairmile or to land co-operatives in Cornwall and the West Country. Those who retired to normal lives to lick their wounds will never be the same: how could you be after you have learnt to build a home for less than forty quid?

Despite its flaws, Pure Genius was a remarkable achievement. It held a multinational to ransom for months and raised the heat of the debate on the current housing crisis by presenting a viable alternative to needlessly carving up the countryside. Architects, planners and UN representatives visited the site and included their findings in reports and new agendas.

In the main, the settlement received warm press coverage and brought a sense of community back to a fractured London borough as well as throwing some of the best parties of the summer.

"The issue is not whether we win or lose," said Green Dave on the night before the eviction, "it is all part of a wider struggle, a wider movement. To create a forest you plant thousands of trees; some may die and some may live, but eventually the forest will grow. Maybe this is one of the trees which never made it, but it has sent ripple effects across Britain and the rest of the world."

Nicola Graydon is a writer, photographer, traveller and spiritual explorer.

Dig the Old Dreams, Man!

ANDREW RIGBY

In 1969 Andrew Rigby was based in Birmingham where he had just started a research project exploring the growth of intentional communities in Britain.

In those days grants and scholarships were more readily available than nowadays, and the process that led me to study communes was not all that different from the processes that led others to live communally. The communes movement was a part of a wider social and cultural movement with which I identified and which embraced various 'alternative' initiatives. In Birmingham there was the Handsworth Free School, the Birmingham Arts Lab, and the Free University of Birmingham. There was the music scene, the alternative press, the food co-ops, and the urban communes, as well as those groups planning to move out of the city to establish rural communes. Birmingham, like other places in Britain during this period (and elsewhere, of course) had its own 'alternative' movement, a general movement of cultural resistance and change – a counter-culture – with which large swathes of young people, especially educated middle class youth, identified to a greater or lesser extent. This was a movement associated with style – style as in fashion, but also style as in lifestyle, the notion that how one lived everyday life and related to others was the most significant dimension of any revolutionary project to save the world.

This was a period when a generation of young people had been radicalised by the Vietnam War – the most barbarous and insane manifestation of a deeply damaged socio-economic and political order. But where was the alternative? No one with an ounce of humanity within them could advocate the model of state socialism presented by the USSR and its totalitarian satellites. And if there was an alternative, how could it be brought into being? How to achieve a sane society?

For many of us the old vision of class conflict as the motor of change was outdated. In that period of relative affluence in the West it seemed that people were trapped not so much by the bonds of economic exploitation but by the silken threads of consumerism. As such, we argued, significant changes needed to take place not merely in the legal ownership of the means of production, but at the deeper level of consciousness. The revolutionary project started with oneself, in the here-and-now. It was our responsibility, not that of some vanguard party, to recreate our lives and our relationships, and to build alternative institutions that embodied the counter-cultural values of co-operation, mutual aid, and self-fulfilment.

Andrew Rigby's seminal work on communes, first published in 1974.

I feel self-conscious now, as I reflect back on that time, but it was a period of messianic hopes. We really did believe that we could remake the world anew, and build Blake's New Jerusalem. And at the forefront of this movement were the communes and the commune-dwellers. They were not just week-end drop-outs, they were living the revolution! They were not just talking (or writing) about it, they were doing it! They were the cells of the new world, exemplars of an alternative way of living which, along with all the other alternative institutions, would wean folk away from the old corrupt patterns so that the old world would eventually collapse in on itself for lack of support.

I was not so much a 'do-er', I was more an observer. (A polite way of putting it!) Throughout the late '60s and early 1970s I travelled round visiting as many communes as I could. In 1971 the annual Directory of Communes, the forerunner of 'Diggers and Dreamers', listed some 40 ventures, but I think a more accurate estimate of the number of self-defined communes or intentional communities in Britain at that time was nearer one hundred. It was a heterogeneous scene. I recall the stereotypical dopeheads talking about 'vibrations' and the mystical union with the universe to be attained through acid. Damaged people also come to mind, lonely souls searching for some kind of sanctuary that would shield them from the harsh straight world. There were also the politicos, the anarchists and the pacifists, who had arrived at communes via the peace movement and various forms of community action, and who sought to live out their protest rather than just demonstrate on the streets at weekends. And then there were the professionals – social workers, teachers and the like – who were committed to their careers but sought alternative living arrangements to the isolation and irrationality of semi-detached suburbia.

As a sociologist I tried to make sense of these people and their world. I ended up with a series of ideal-types, analytical constructs which highlighted the range of communes and which was based upon the different intentions or motives underpinning the various ventures. I arrived at a six-fold classification (or set of coat-hangers) upon which I based my observations.

1 Self-actualising communes: Communities which were viewed primarily as settings within which the members could develop their self-awareness and realise their true selves. The members were often the archetypal hippies, seeking escape from the constraints of the mundane world and the freedom to 'do their own thing'. The talk was very much of freedom, the individual and the self. Frequently such ventures started life as unintentional communities – a bunch of people living together – but then someone would come along and identify them as a commune, and they would begin to take

the label on as their own. I recall that the commune at Eel Pie Island near Twickenham started off in such a manner. Such ventures were prone to collapse as people moved on to new places and new pursuits, but some have survived – Shrubb (now Shrub) Family for one.

2 Activist communes: The members of such communes viewed their project primarily in terms of providing a base from which they could involve themselves in neighbourhood politics and wider community action. For some reason a surprising number of the people I encountered within these 'red bases' had been involved with the Student Christian Movement at college, and had been active with the Young Liberals! They were much more obviously 'political' than the freedom-seekers and dope-heads in the self-actualising communes and, given my background, I felt far more at ease with them.

Forty people lived in the dilapidated hotel on Eel Pie Island in mid-Thames, near Richmond.

3 Practical communes: The members of these
ventures defined their project primarily in
terms of the practical advantages to be
achieved through cooperative living – sharing
facilities and engaging in common activities
for pleasure and profit. As I think back to the
visits I made to such communities now, what
comes to mind is Ilkley! A nice place to visit,
look in the shops, wander on the moor – but
would you really want to live in a place so
heavily dominated by the professional and
middle classes? Should not a healthy community embrace a wider cross-section of society
than teachers, local government officers and
civil engineers?

4 Therapeutic communes: Controlled environments with healing properties where people
suffering from one or more kinds of handicap
could live a life within which they might ful-
fil their potential as human beings. There
were, and are, a wide range of such communities – stretching from the relatively formal
and structured Camphill Communities
through to much 'looser' communes where
the distinction between carers and their
'charges' was fuzzy to say the least.

5 Communes for mutual support: These were
communities within which the members
sought to achieve a sense of fellowship and
experience a degree of mutual support unat-
tainable in the conventional world, dominated as it was by competitive individualism and
intolerance of deviance. I have to confess that
when I think back to those ventures that
approximated most closely to this ideal-type,
the image that comes back through the mists
of time is of lonely people; people who had
been damaged in some way or another by
society; people who, because of their sexual
orientation or some other aspect of their lives,
found it impossible to be 'at home' in the conventional world dominated by the social insti-
tution of the nuclear family.

6 Religious communes: These were the communities whose wider purpose was defined by members in the context of some supra-mundane or sacred power. Members might have viewed themselves as living a divinely-ordained life in community, or living within the kind of environment which heightened the possibilities of directly experiencing the divine. Alongside the recollections of the deeply Christian lay communities I visited, I have the memory of visiting the Findhorn Community when there were only about 16 people living there, and about five of them were visitors. I felt very important as Peter Caddy explained to me that as a writer and researcher I had a valuable function to perform in spreading the word about the Centre of Light that he and his family and friends were establishing.

For the purposes of my research I found it useful to characterise communes according to the dominant 'intention' that had informed their formation. In practice, of course, no commune could ever be adequately characterised along such a unidimensional plane. Communes are made up of their members, and the members bring to the project their own particular dreams, goals and traumas. As the membership changes, so does the character of the commune. Nothing stays constant – although I find it surprising when I scan through contemporary directories of communes in Britain, just how many of them date their origins back to the 1960s and early 1970s. The institutions have survived, but how many have retained their messianic conviction?

In the harsh economic climate of recent years, it is all too easy to dismiss the alternative society movement of the late 1960s as little more than the empty symbolic posturing of disaffected but relatively privileged middle class youth. Certainly, when they show repeats of the old Woodstock movie on television these days, I am sure I am not alone amongst my generation (no pun intended) in cringing at some of the scenes.

OK, maybe in emphasising the revolutionary significance of lifestyle we attributed too much importance to a movement that for many was merely a movement of fashion, rather than a sustained attempt to transform the very roots of domination and exploitation in our society. And yes, maybe the challenge to the work ethic that was an integral part of the counter culture was little more than a celebration of idleness by those whose age and communal lifestyle allowed them to escape the exigencies of earning a living, albeit temporarily. There was a strong element of cultural elitism about the counter cultural movement, a failure to engage with the concerns of the 'ordinary working people'. When one believed that consciousness was the critical variable, it was too easy to slip into believing that domination and exploitation could be transcended merely by thinking differently. There was an unhealthy narcissism in much of the focusing upon the significance of the self, to the exclusion of any concern with wider issues. In practice, the elevation of 'doing your own thing' into a prime value resulted in people becoming victim to every passing whim and failing to respect the rights of others – a discrepancy between rhetoric and practice which was particularly marked in relation to the treatment of women within the institutions of the alternative society.

> **It was a time of enormous creativity which stemmed from the utopian confidence that anything was possible**

And yet, despite all these negative attributes, it was much more than this. It was a wonderful time when, in a way that it is hard to imagine now, considerable numbers of people enjoyed the space and the opportunity to experiment with their lives. It was a time of enormous creativity which stemmed from the utopian confidence that anything was possible. Moreover, it was during this period that the conception of struggle was deepened beyond a concern with class to embrace issues of identity and patterns of domination in all spheres of life.

However hedonistic and self-centred the period and the movement might appear when viewed in retrospect, most of those involved in communes and the wider alternative society movement of that time saw no disjunction between the process of transforming their own life and the wider object of changing the world. It was all part of the same seamless project. And that message is as relevant today as it ever was.

Andrew Rigby wrote **Alternative Realities** and **Communes in Britain** – two of the best known works on communal living in the 1970s. He teaches in the Department of Peace Studies at the University of Bradford and is review editor of *Peace News*.

POST CA

Tuesday, Dear Jane,

Ok – I know Frank and I are keen on this community lark (well, he is!), but I'm beginning to wonder if rural solitude doesn't turn people a little nuts. Or maybe it's too many lentils! You know I told you we were visiting communes (sorry, communities!) for tips on how to set up our own? So we wrote to this place in Sussex: could we come down and stay overnight, ask questions, wash up, feed the chickens? Letter comes back: overjoyed to have you, please come, meet you off the train – sounded great! So we get there Friday night. Great big brick house, cold, people in woollies huddled in front of wood stoves, lots of knitting going on. Stockpot soup and nettle crumble for supper (don't ask!). So we bring out our list of questions, they look a bit cross, grunt a bit – and at 9.30, they all piss off to bed. All of them! Keep the fire in, they said! Saturday – similar. They're all out stringing up an electric pig fence. Lentil bake, chocolate rock cakes, camomile tea, bed. Will we become those people if we do this?

Love, Emily

A wintry scene at Brighton Naturist Beach
(photo: Hugo van Wadenogen)

Book Review

Sarah Eno (a former member of Crabapple and Laurieston Hall) reviews:
The Commune
a novel by **Margaret Buckley**

ISBN: 0 897765 00 2
Chrysalis Press, 1993 ● 386pp paperback ● £9
(available from "Edge of Time Ltd" for £10 including p&p, see page 224)

Mark (who is retiring early from academia), Sheila and their three children buy a house and land to farm organically. Another couple, Bess and Tom who are finishing a book join them. At some point a colleague of Mark's arrives, ostensibly to write an article but intrigued by him and the group she returns along with several other people also from academia, for the summer holidays. Bess and Tom's teenage daughter and her boyfriend appear; friends come round for dinner and a rather unsavoury neighbouring family act as a foil for the ideals of Mark. So far, fairly familiar. The barest of opening scenes is set, but thereafter no stage directions and few descriptions of people or objects are given.

The prose style flows endlessly through a stream of incidents – Mark confronting the neighbour, Tom learning to plough, Bess and Joan sitting over breakfast, after dinner conversations with visitors, the group outing to the house of a famous author, the flattened grass where a couple had lain together, musical events, yoga sessions – all are grist to the mill for a detailed examination of the minutiae of the characters emotional condition and responses to each other, to the events of daily life.

Sheila seems to do all the cooking with occasional help. Mark pretty much has the ideas and runs the place and everyone else helps with the land work when asked or when they feel like doing it. The commune becomes a vehicle in which to explore the problems of being human; to reveal the confusions, contradictions and incoherence of everyday life.

Many recognisable themes are there: the need for love yet fear of intimacy, to belong yet retain independence, the need for mental and emotional balance. for a harmony which fuels energy, for freedom and spontaneity, a life where feeling aid thinking are one, where humans act rightly because they are in touch wtth their instincts, "like dolphins".

Many important and interesting ideas are presented, sometimes discussed and argued at length but never explored in practice. "For me this is the only freedom worth having", says Mark. "This way most of our objectives are physical and achievable and because of that we get back a sense of possibilities. Here the powerlessness goes and because of that the objectives become not just physical but, once they're shared, carriers of emotional and imaginative connotations giving rise to new ideas and attitudes that might slowly affect the world". "We need to feel excited and alive and that somehow we belong and are doing something worthwhile".

Although it is hinted, largely through Mark, that the commune is the place where these can find resolution there is little exploration of the successes and failures within the communal structure. Does anyone really feel that communal living is empowering them, that it is worthwhile, that they are getting close to instinctive action? What is it that the commune really offers? It is full of potential but is anything realised? Is intimacy and belonging without engendering fear and jealousy possible? It is hinted at and there is retreat and finally tragedy . Is that the author's answer?

Issues of co-operation, concensus, building liberating yet organised moral and social systems are raised but they are always remote from the group's own life. There is no dealing with those gripping and contentious questions of power, ownership, decision-making, income generation, pets, sharing the tasks or any other practicalities of living communally which really test the strength of the fantasies we can so easily dream.

The connection between the personal and political is acknowledged, and the personal is explored in intense detail and at great depth but somehow the implications are not really grasped. Perhaps that is because the author refuses to be objective, to present a coherent picture from the outside but stays hidden within the narrative. In fact as a reader one feels at times as if one has accidentally dropped in on other people's lives and whilst that is quite powerful the lack of documentation or analysis also leaves the reader outside the action.

So I feel the book is more about Mark's search for answers to questions that should be or may be important and relevant to many of us. And by using a group of people who are to some extent living and working together the author takes us on an intense and quite serious journey through a philosophical and moral maze about the emotional nature of ourselves when pushed a bit, but without really getting to grips with the communal aspects. So, read it for the close, sometimes exhausting observation of emotional lives rather than an exploration of an exciting lifestyle.

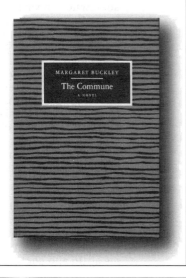

MARGARET BUCKLEY

The Commune
A NOVEL

Cycles of Change in Kibbutzim

DAVE DARBY

Between two visits to Israel separated by a number of years,

Dave Darby experienced life in dozens of different communities

around the world. In this article he describes what he found on his

return to Israel ... after cycling from England!

I arrived in Haifa on a boat from Crete, and cycled to a café to phone an Israeli friend I'd met in the Philippines, and who'd invited me to stay at his place if I ever visited Israel again. I knew he lived in Qiryat Yam, which was somewhere near Haifa, but I had no idea how to get there. I had no change, so I asked the guy behind the counter, whereupon came the stark reminder that I was back in Israel, a land whose people are much maligned for their rudeness, but who in my view are merely misunderstood. The person in question looked up from his paper, eyed me up and down, growled 'No!', and carried on reading. I shrugged my shoulders, found someone else with change, and made the call, which wasn't easy, as my friend wasn't there, and I had to try and understand the scanty directions given by his mother, whose English was about as good as my Hebrew. When I'd finished, my friend with the newspaper shouted 'Hey!', and gestured me over. He'd overheard my call, and so spent the next 10 minutes drawing me a detailed map of how to get to my destination, after which he totally ignored me again and continued reading. That said it all really. He wasn't able to help me with change, so why elaborate? When he could help me, he did. In a similar way, I'd seen kibbutzniks who were so short with each other that I thought they were arguing, when in fact they were enquiring after each other's health.

The development of the kibbutzim is inextricably linked to the influx of Jews to Palestine, which was initially fired by oppression and pogroms in Russia and Eastern Europe, which escalated after the first Russian Revolution. The land was not settled in the typical individualistic 'pioneer' way for four main reasons[1].

1
Co-operation in Israel and the World by Dr Walter Preuss. Rubin Mass, Jerusalem, 1967.

● Individual capitalists would have found it cheaper to use local Arab labour, leaving no room for Jewish settlers.

● All the settlers were united in their Jewishness and experiences of oppression.

● Most of the settlers were urbanites, and only through collective settlements could the majority learn from the few who were farmers.

● After the Revolution, many had a natural affinity for socialist ideals from their life experiences in Russia and Eastern Europe.

Dr Franz Oppenheimer, a German university lecturer, was one of the first to suggest co-operative settlements to the Zionist movement, in 1904, and the first kibbutz – Degania Aleph – was founded in 1908. In 1920, the first Kibbutz Federation – The United Kibbutz Movement, or TAKAM – was formed, and since then, the movement has expanded to encompass 130,000 people in 269 kibbutzim[2].

2
Kibbutz Facts and Figures, a pamphlet issued by Yad Tabenkin. Research and Documentation Centre of the United Kibbutz Movement, PO Ramat Efal, Israel 52960, 1994.

So the history of co-operation in Israel was not a revolt against capitalism, but the result of special circumstances – not theoretical, but practical – to settle the land.

Kibbutz Gezer

I cycled 150 km from just north of Haifa, to Kibbutz Gezer, which is situated mid-way between Tel Aviv and Jerusalem.

Memories of my previous stay on a kibbutz eight years ago came flooding back to me as I queued to serve myself breakfast. Kibbutz food is wonderful: soft cheeses, aubergines, avocados, fruit, olives, houmous. Before breakfast I'd been working, pulling weeds out of the compost heaps, and now I was off to help decorate a house for a new member. At lunchtime I re-familiarised myself with that other ubiquitous and most welcome kibbutz feature – the swimming pool – after which, before going back to work, I took my bike along to the workshop of the resident bicycle fanatic, as it had developed a few strange noises recently. During my stay he changed just about every bearing on the bike so that when I left it was like floating on air.

3
Such as **Kibbutz Trends**, a quarterly journal published by **Yad Tabenkin** under the auspices of the Federation of Kibbutz Movements.

At Gezer, through talking to kibbutzniks and reading any literature I found lying around[3], I began to understand what was happening to the kibbutzim. It seemed that their idealism had been severely diluted, and that the emphasis was moving from the communal to the individual. Meals were often taken in private now, and there was talk of wage differentials, for example, which would have been considered heresy even a few years ago. Thatcherism had arrived on the kibbutz scene! Something that had already happened was that several kibbutzim had floated shares in their factories. I wanted to talk to my friend about this apparent lurch towards the conventional in the kibbutz movement.

First he told me a little about this kibbutz. It's part of the TAKAM group of kibbutzim, although he did say that with the recent changes, differences between the different kibbutz groups had become minimal. TAKAM for example, were the first to phase out separate children's accommodation, which had become unpopular with kids and parents alike, but in the last few years, the Artzi federation had followed suit. Financially there have

Is the communal dining-room threatened by the changes taking place in the Kibbutz system?

been differences though. In the 80's, TAKAM kibbutzim lost a lot of money through financial speculation, but the more ideological Artzi kibbutzim dabbled less and so fared much better.

There is a General Assembly of all members every couple of weeks or so, and committees are elected to deal with specific areas. Basically, if there's an issue that needs to be dealt with on a day-to-day basis, a committee is elected to deal with it. There are rules, but within boundaries set by the kibbutz organisation. In practice, though, most decisions are made over coffee by the people involved.

There are advantages in belonging to an organization as big as the kibbutz movement. You can buy in bulk and arrange bigger loans under better terms. And then there are the trouble-shooters. Certain individuals have positions within the movement which involve sorting out difficulties for individual kibbutzim using the power of the whole movement as a lever. The example quoted to me was that of a kibbutz dealing with a company which was dragging its feet in repairing a certain weighbridge which was vital to the functioning of the kibbutz. A troubleshooter was contacted and he informed the company that all cheques from the movement would be withheld nationwide until the weighbridge was fixed. Needless to say, it did the trick.

Although nominally, of course, the kibbutzim are Jewish communities, you don't have to be Jewish to live on Gezer. Jewish festivals are celebrated together, but in the secular kibbutzim there are no religious ceremonies, and what you do in you own house is your business.

My friend wasn't too happy that pragmatism seems to be replacing ideology in the kibbutzim, and he thinks that the move towards the autonomy of the individual will mean an end to the 'one-purse' principle, and that members will get bank cards and individual accounts soon.

A more benevolent wind of change blowing through the kibbutz movement was pointed out to me – that of environmental awareness, and the 'greening' of agriculture and industry – which my friend is very much involved with, both locally at Gezer, and initiating environmental policies for the whole movement. Gezer has a group called 'the Environmental Crew', who run programmes with a different theme each month. Past themes have included composting, recycling and transport, and they have a 5000 shekel budget for education from central funds. Although neither Gezer nor any other kibbutz is completely organic, spraying has been drastically reduced here, and there is a plan to meter electricity use for individual households to try and reduce consumption. As children from outside attend the kindergarten here, and they receive a liberal dose of environmental propaganda, it is hoped that they can help to influence activity in the local area as well as on the kibbutz.

Nationally, my friend was influential in setting up the 'Green Room' – an office and seminar centre in Tel Aviv – to co-ordinate and stimulate environmental action in the kibbutz movement. They plan to develop an official environmental department for the movement, and they have already hosted well-attended meetings where plans were discussed to formulate national environmental policy, to bring kibbutz members together with Palestinian groups to work on joint projects, and to set up a model ecological kibbutz, probably Gezer.

A kibbutznik has founded SPNI – an organic farming organization in Israel, similar to the Soil Association in Britain – and now 66 kibbutzim are registered as having at least some of their fields farmed organically. Kibbutz volunteers from abroad can now specify that they would like to be sent to one of these kibbutzim, and my friend has written to Lionel Pollard in Australia to be included in the next international Willing Workers On Organic Farms directory. The SPNI has said that the fastest way to change Israeli society is via the kibbutzim, and in the past up to 40% of politicians have been drawn from this 2% of the population at any one time. The kibbutzim will play a pivotal role in any change in Israel. Having settled the land it now has to green the country, to attract forward-thinking people and regain its role in the vanguard of Israeli society.

During my stay at Gezer I made a trip to Yad Tabenkin, the International Communes Desk and information centre, which produces *CALL*, a quarterly newsletter for and about international communities. The place is run by Shlomo Shalmon and Yaacov Oved, who I'd first met when he delivered a paper at the international communities conference in Edinburgh in 1988. I spent an afternoon browsing their library which must be the world's biggest collection of literature on co-operative living.

Peace is something that is high on the agenda at Gezer. One evening I was invited to a poolside gathering of young kibbutzniks, Palestinians and foreigners. We swam, practised Jewish and Palestinian folk dancing, and sat around to discuss the Arab-Israeli problem. The discussions were positive, although I suppose that just by being there, the Palestinian delegation was accepting a Jewish presence in Palestine (if not the existence of a Jewish state) which is a bottom line for any constructive dialogue. The linking of any state with any religion is beyond my comprehension, but maybe one day Jews, Muslims, Christians and non-believers will live together in a secular, democratic Middle East. And pigs might fly? Well, at least the politicians have begun to talk, although I'd feel much more optimistic if the young people at Gezer were in charge.

Kibbutz Harduf

I particularly wanted to see Harduf, as it is an Anthroposophic kibbutz, ie following the philosophy of Rudolf Steiner, and as well, it is a long way down the path of privatisation. I found my contact Varda Shilo, and her two granddaughters showed me to my room. After talking with them for a while I was astonished to find out that they weren't Irish, but that they were born and bred in Israel, a country whose accent is usually virtually impossible to lose; but these two spoke perfect colloquial English with a thick Irish brogue after studying there for only a couple of years. As there was a problem to find any work for me to do here, I was charged for the room, so to save money I decided to stay only for a day or two, just

Members accommodation in idyllic surroundings at Kibbutz Dan. How long before there are fences around each house, and a car in each driveway?

enough time to have a look around and have a chat with Varda. She explained the set-up to me, and it seemed at first that this was about as far as you could go and still be a kibbutz. On other kibbutzim, for example, it's often said that members are using the communal dining-room less and less these days, but on Harduf they don't even have one. However, there is no voting here; all decisions are made by consensus, and there is a spiritual focus which means – so I was told – that there isn't the gossip and backbiting that you'll find on other kibbutzim.

Harduf was founded in 1982 by a group of 15, many of whom had lived in or visited Findhorn in Scotland. Now there are 39 families living here, 80% coming from the Kibbutz Artzi Federation. They have a bakery, biodynamic agriculture, a dairy herd, a Waldorf school, two kindergartens, a clinic and a drug rehabilitation centre, funded partly by the government. All of these businesses are owned by the kibbutz, but this is where the similarity with other kibbutzim ends. Apart from the consensus decision-making and the lack of communal dining room, Harduf is not income-sharing, and as well as the community forum once a week, each business has independent meetings. The kibbutz doesn't pay for anything on behalf of the members; accommodation, electricity and water are paid for from members' private incomes. On other kibbutz there is usually an age limit of 38 for new members. Here there is no such limit. Finally, the whole place is organic.

It's not an easy kibbutz to join. First you have to show a commitment to Anthroposophy, which involves a two-year study period before being accepted as a full member. For this reason, it's impossible to compare this kibbutz to others. There is a different consciousness here which underlines their lifestyle and the bonds between people. Co-operation is not the only focus.

Harduf represents an interesting new development in the kibbutz movement, but for me it was strange and rather sad to see private cars parked next to houses on internal roads.

Tepee village

At Gezer, I was told, I would find a community of people living in tepees and I wouldn't have much difficulty finding it because the tepees were situated around the top of a hill and were visible from many miles away. This was true. I could pick out three or four tiny white triangles on the rather barren, scrubby hillside about two hours before I eventually reached them, which represented about 20 miles, as I was steadily climbing with the wind against me.

I was surprised to see a 2 metre high wall of earth that had been piled across the track from the road up to the village, over which I managed, with difficulty, to drag myself and my bike. I arrived at the same time as two villagers who had been into the nearest town to get food, and had returned with a box of less-than-fresh vegetables that local market traders hadn't managed to sell by the time the market closed for the day, and would otherwise have thrown away. I was offered tea, and invited to sit around a fire further on up the hill. It turned out that the land here was owned, not co-operatively, but by a benevolent landlord who lived in Tel Aviv, and who visited from time to time.

When I visited there were four people looking after the place permanently, but when members return from their various trips, numbers fluctuate between 10 and 20. Work involves chopping wood, maintenance, cooking, composting and growing a few vegetables such as radishes and tomatoes. The emphasis is definitely on relaxation though, and there is a 'magic hat' into which members and guests can contribute to cover costs, which don't amount to much as they like to live very simply. There were five full-sized tepees, and there were plans to create a yoga centre and to get linked to the mains water supply, after which it was hoped that the people who are away at the moment will come back and settle. I spent the night in a tepee and was greeted in the morning with a delicious breakfast consisting of a stew of soya, tomatoes and chickpeas, before heading off further north into Galilee. I had to climb over the huge mound of earth again, which I discovered had been put there by some of the locals, who had always been hostile towards them, inspired by predictable and entirely false stories in local rags of sex orgies and the like, although why that should have bothered them even if they were true, I don't know.

I found the people here very friendly and welcoming, and their community was certainly extremely wild and beautiful, but I had the impression that this was never going to be more than a transitory community – especially as its very existence depended on the continued benevolence of an absentee landlord – but that's probably what they wanted. I felt that their motivation was less about really trying to change society, and more to do with hanging out and having a good time – not that there's anything wrong with that. Some of the visitors here were very familiar characters, posing as the rebels they quite obviously weren't. Sure enough, on my return to England I received a letter from a young Israeli woman I'd met there who informed me that the landlord's philanthropy had suddenly dried up, and so I suppose they would all have to go off and find somewhere else to hang out.

Kibbutz Dan
I cycled in a 140km arc past the Sea of Galilee and up towards the Golan Heights, at the foot of which I would find the nature reserve containing the ancient city of Dan, and its neighbouring kibbutz of the same name, where I'd been a volunteer worker for six months, eight years previously.

There I met again Amicham, an expert on land drainage, who had been involved in draining the Upper Galilee marshes and turning them into super-productive farmland. The thing that I remembered most about him was that he'd been hired to do some work on the Panama Canal. He had unique specialist knowledge for which he was paid almost a million dollars for two years' work, after which he returned to Dan and put his earnings into the collective fund. If more kibbutzniks showed such unselfish commitment to the kibbutz ideal, then there wouldn't be any doubts about the movement's survival – doubts I heard expressed several times during this trip; doubts that weren't there eight years ago (to my knowledge).

Late one evening, for example, I met Yarif and Shelley walking with their baby. Shelley pointed to the children playing on the grass and said what a wonderful lifestyle it was. It was almost 11 at night, yet parents didn't have to worry about them. The area was well-lit, and there was no danger from cars or from other people. Yarif agreed, but said that in his opinion each kibbutz was too big to allow members to feel a real responsibility for it, and that this lack of personal responsibility could presage the demise of the whole movement.

People now don't have the same motivation as the original settlers

People now don't have the same motivation as the original settlers, certainly. The kibbutz movement at first defied all Smithian economic rationality, because rationality doesn't encompass idealism. The pioneers sang and danced whilst working hard for very little personal reward, because they were forging the state of Israel. Now that Israel exists, a new motivation is needed – capitalist society can offer greater rewards for skilled people. One solution is for the government to give tax breaks for the kibbutzim, but I can't see this happening. Most people in Israel don't live in kibbutzim, and their central role in settling the land has gone, so it would probably be a vote loser. If people want to leave to make more money elsewhere, then I say let them go – the kibbutz movement would be smaller, but better off without them. The drive to settle Israel created an artificially large communal movement, and now that drive has gone, the movement must either shrink whilst retaining its ideology, or change. I suggest that shrinking would be preferable, but change is what actually seems to be happening.

As well as the movement being too large to maintain its ideology, there may also be a case for suggesting that individual kibbutzim are too big. In an ideal community, there should be no need to talk of incentives; instead it should operate like a big family, which in my experience is impossible when the number of members exceeds 100. As the average kibbutz consists of over 500 individuals, there is a tendency for people to begin to ask, 'what can I get from this community?', instead of, 'what can I contribute to this community?'

For this same reason, the Ujamaa communities in Tanzania (average size around 3,000 people) had to press for the government to pass a law enabling them to evict members who were quite willing to avail themselves of the communally provided services, but refused to pull their weight. Apart from this, a community of 500 people would find it virtually impossible to come to any decisions via consensus, which would almost inevitably lead to factions and in-fighting.

Obviously, smaller kibbutzim couldn't support large-scale industry, but it would be possible to organise a collaborative effort between several kibbutzim, which would open up various possibilities: businesses could be located in towns, and be registered as separate co-ops – even involving workers from outside the kibbutz movement. This would provide opportunities to forge links with local communities, as well as just within the kibbutz network. As it is, the intensity, and the drive to increase efficiency and profits in kibbutz industry means that work can often be dreary and monotonous. Although members rotate jobs every three years, how enthusiastic can you get about working six days a week in a sprinkler factory for three years? Kibbutz members don't tend to enjoy the range of work that members of small communities do. The main reason this situation has come about is over-investment in the past, leading to debt. Rotation of managers led to a situation whereby managers in new positions wanted to prove themselves quickly, so would borrow to implement their new ideas. Even if the investments were bad and created nothing but debt, the kibbutz being what it is, the managers wouldn't lose their jobs. The size of the kibbutz movement also means that debts can be covered: total debts in 1994 amounted to four billion US dollars (US$ 33,000 per head.) Consequently, there has had to be a re-evaluation of kibbutz industrial organisation to attempt to pay off the debt. Kibbutz Ein Zevam in the Golan has introduced differential pay based on skill levels, and although the land and equipment is still collectively owned, TAKAM are discussing whether they've gone too far to still be considered a member.

Kibbutzim may not find it as easy to secure loans in the future however, but looked at from the perspective of maintaining the co-operative ideology, this may not be a bad thing.

There is a new phenomenon in the kibbutz movement though, where the original idealism is alive and well, and that is urban kibbutzim. This is essentially an experiment, involving mainly younger people, in much smaller communities of around 10-20 individuals, who see part of their role as helping to regenerate slum areas of cities. They tend to buy up unused apartment blocks, which are divided up into members rooms and communal areas. They all have outside jobs from which income is pooled, and they host study evenings to which any interested outsiders are welcome.

I think that there are two possible paths that the kibbutz movement may take. Either de-collectivisation will continue apace until there is only a blurred distinction with conventional industries and agriculture, if any at all. People will begin to have their own bank accounts, cars and hourly rates of pay. Factories may be bought by private owners and kibbutz members employed in them. Even kibbutz houses could be bought privately and the kitchen done away with. Or, new and splinter kibbutzim could be smaller and greener and retain the original collective ideals.

In reality I think that both these things will happen, so that now that the special circumstances surrounding the birth of the kibbutz movement no longer exist, the communal sector will settle out to around the level found in other Western countries, and then begin to expand again – in Israel as well as everywhere else.

Dave Darby is currently putting together a book on communal living in twenty different countries. Born and brought up in Dudley, West Midlands, he now lives at Redfield Community, and presents a slide show on communities around the world, during their regular "Living in Communities" weekends.

POST CA

Thursday, Dear Jane,
Ok – I know the whole thing about living in communities is
that everyone pitches in and holds up their end and all that –
I read it in **Diggers and Dreamers** so it must be true.
Anyway, we went to a community near Hereford last
weekend, and Friday night at supper everyone talks about how
they all do maintenance together so they can help each other
and share skills and how any job can be fun if you're doing it
with other people. Great! So just before lunchtime Saturday
they lead us into the woods and there's this green plasticky
thing humming away, and it's full of shit – literally! It's called a
bio-digester or something, and it's where all the sewage goes
because of course they're not on the mains. Needs cleaning out,
they said. Frank goes white as a sheet when they take the
top off, but we start in with three of the comrades – and
then after fifteen minutes they kind of melt away and it
takes us three hours and then another three hours in the
shower to get the smell off, and we found out later that our
mentors had spent a happy lunch hour in the pub! Can
communities be exploitative? Discuss ...
Love, Emily

The modern headquarters building of Offa's Dyke Water plc
Mappa Mundi Business Park, Hereford

Grow your own  Commune

SARAH BUNKER

Should communes be more like ecosystems?

Just how organic dare we be?

Planting the Seed

Communes come from dreams: but they do become real. And when they become real, they start to grow and evolve in quite an organic way.

That strange birth, from ideas and desires, is a fragile process; most communes fail before they reach reality, and it isn't surprising. Organising the initial assembly of people, ideas, money and space/shelter is exhausting and nerve-wracking. So many dreams and so much security is often on the line, and the more there is to lose, or gain, the more fearful yet exhilarating the trip becomes.

The Need for Time

Any complex collection of organisms, like a forest or a coral reef, has been getting it together for an awfully long time, yet if we want to create sustainable communities of people, we need to make them complex, adaptable and robust, just like natural systems – and do it in a few years. Those who have attempted to recreate ecosystems from scratch have found that it's not simply a matter of throwing in the ingredients and watching it take shape. Natural communities form over a long period of time – and we're talking oceans of time here, not just a few months. Communities of people likewise need time to come into being.

Secondly, what you might regard as a 'mature' ecosystem is not just an older version of how it started: it's quite a different thing, and has been arrived at by a succession of different organisms, 'pioneer' species (like birch trees) preparing the way (not in any conscious way) for those that follow (like oaks). Some might argue that this happens in commune building, too; the community may be quite different from its early days, the founder member types having given way to the steady member types (or having evolved into them), who then carry the project forward in its 'mature' state.

Not only do the parts of the prospective commune have to arrive in the right amounts and in the right order, but there may also be a key element which will kick the whole thing into existence; something as romantic as a chance meeting between people with similar dreams, or as practical as the sudden appearance of an investor. As if all this is not difficult enough, there is the added problem of actually inventing something from scratch; not recreating an already existing, evolving system as we find in nature, but taking the ideas in our heads and making them real.

Cartoon by Massimo

Life, Death and Evolution in the Commune

Although some communes are intentionally anarchist, many are a tension-forming emulsion of individual anarchist and control freak tendencies where everyone really wants things to happen by themselves – but in a sort of controlled way! Two things which may prevent communes from embracing more anarchy are:

1 people bringing fears and experience of anarchy, as generally perceived, into the commune and,

2 the need for the commune to interface with the 'outside'. This need to interact with the wider society necessitates some structures, which, depending on design, can be good or bad.

For communes to become really 'organic', control has to come about from the bottom up, as a form of anarchy or endarchy (government from within) – and that means not only from within the group of individuals making up the commune, but also from within the whole soup of collective ideals, which nurture equality, co-operation and respect, and seek solutions which do not rely on hierarchies.

"So," the stranger asked, "who is in charge here?" and the commune grinned from ear to ear.

No-one is in charge but everyone is, has to be the mark of a real grassroots organisation. The commune in this case is a distributed being; each individual is part of that being and inputs into the control of the whole beast. Whether you could call such a collective an organism is difficult to say, perhaps such things are more like swarms or corals or meadows in the strength of their connections and the unison of their actions. But such a distributed being does have a number of attributes, which allows something to be created which is greater than the sum of its parts.

attributes, which allows something to be created which is greater than the sum of its parts.

Such a decentralised system relies heavily on communication, and on redundancy of information. Ideally, information is constantly being passed around, mutating here and there (sometimes accidentally, sometimes not!), getting corrected (sometimes), but always with enough people and moving fast enough to be up to date and of use to the situation at hand. The sort of massive redundancy which is created in this process may seem inefficient, but information is cheap and (relatively) easy – we can store a lot of day-to-day knowledge in our collective heads, creating insurance against loss, and the ability to re-route around problems.

Redundancy is a natural attribute, and so is parallelism, a process which smooths the action in an organic context. Using a parallel approach to problem solving, several individuals tackle a problem at the same time (brainstorming is a great example), which often results in fast, elegant and sometimes unexpected solutions, unlike the clunky clockwork-like sequential approach so notorious in very large conventional institutions.

The weirdest attribute of a collective is that it is more than the sum of its parts. Energy is created seemingly out of nothing and something comes out of it which is totally unexpected. Some argue that, in organisms, consciousness may be such an emergent thing. We may expect communities to likewise throw off some novel attribute; perhaps a totally new form of culture, born of developing new co-operative ways of working together. For me, it is the sense or spirit of community which is that strange emergent thing, and it is the taste of it which keeps me living in one.

The complexity of communities can have the effect of freaking out accountants and solicitors who are used to simpler systems, but complexity is, once again, a trademark of natural self-organising systems

ture of the commune. People do any number of different jobs around the place and at any one time hold a subset of the total information. As well as skills, energy and information being decentralised, money and decisions may also be, with kitties for different projects and quick decisions being made by small groups as they work together.

Complexity of this nature reacts badly if mixed with inappropriate bureacracy. This can lead to a nasty case of severe bogged-downness, and a surreal, nightmare quality akin to the Terry Gilliam film, *Brazil*.

Luckily, communes change. Sometimes dramatically via a revolution, but more often in an incremental way via an evolution.

Adaptability is a sort of short-term or 'trial' evolution. It can be very effective, both in creating and in dealing with change, and its effectiveness is amplified by parallel thinking, distributed skills and sub-group decision-making. In the longer term, change happens as the population of individuals changes over the years, and different approaches and solutions are tried.

Obviously it is important for the commune to change as circumstances change, but it doesn't want to be changing every five minutes or reinventing the wheel continually. Rather, continual, gradual, graceful change which is accepted throughout the collective would be the ideal. To achieve this, a certain balance between stability and agitation is needed, with the passing around and mulling over of anecdotes being a way for the group to analyse past decisions. Change is woven into co-operative living but is something so fought against by individuals in western society that it is often difficult to embrace wholeheartedly in the communal setting – change somehow seems to be associated with endings rather than beginnings.

Although it may be exhausting for older members to retry ideas with each new set of residents, because things do change, approaches which did not work before might suddenly be very effective.

It is the pressure to evolve which is one of the most positive aspects of the commune, and allows it to react more quickly than institutions which have been designed with only one set of parameters in mind. The constant experimenting with ideas during the process to invent itself leads to a steep learning curve and, of course, mistakes.

Evolution is nurtured by taking note of such mistakes and adjusting accordingly, and by always investigating the fringes of what is known or experimented with, which entails a certain amount of 'living on the edge', which in this case means being on the edge of control. (Not a happy state for control freaks!) When communes move away from the edge and slip into the comfort zone, the pace of change and evolvability both drop, leading to a slow decline into stagnation.

But is stagnation such a bad thing? With no pressure to change, things sometimes remain in one form for a very long time. With communes, as with nature, it is difficult to define success. Is it that a commune has twenty siblings of ten people each, or that it itself has grown to eight hundred? Is it that it has changed the structure of government or law towards greater equality, or that it serves humanity or the natural systems on which we rely in some other way? Or perhaps it is enough to simply exist as a counter-flow to the general increase in isolation and alienation felt by many in western society.

Reproduction of our complex living organisations probably occurs more often by the passing on of ideas than by a simple budding-off of satellites which carry on the aims of the parent organisations. In this way, the progeny are diverse – unusual fusions of ideas, each containing a nugget of information which says "This is real; this is already working; you too can do this". Subversive reproduction!

And a commune, like organisms and ecologies, affects its environment in a way that nurtures itself. Such positive feedback may take the form of gardening, being involved in local politics and the wider community, and networking with like-minded organisations. Such actions certainly help prepare the way for more communes.

And what about death? It is perfectly natural for a complex self-organising system to die. Sometimes the reason may be apparent, and at other times not. It is better that a commune closes shop and the individuals move on in their lives than they feel tied to a set of ideals which don't seem to be getting anywhere. If it's working, you'll know; a buzz will be in the air and a constant feeling of falling through problems and out the other end, richer for the experience.

That communes exist and that they work for their members and constantly attract new members is no small thing. That there is an alternative is not trivial. That community can be rebuilt is very important. The creation of spaces, small pockets, where a sense of community is being built up rather than eroded, is a sign of a living thing at work.

By emulating the organic world rather than the mechanical, we unleash the power to evolve further than we can at present imagine, and grow the culture of the future.

This article was inspired by Kevin Kelly's excellent and thought-provoking book **Out of Control**, published by Addison Wesley.

Sarah Bunker has lived at Beech Hill Community for eight years. Her favourite topic is composting toilets, and she will happily chat about them at any time – especially at dinner! (She is also very fond of insects.)

Grave Planning Matters

PATRICK UPTON

At Laurieston Hall Community constructing a graveyard for

deceased members was the next item on the agenda

... after fixing the gutters!

Laurieston Hall community is getting older and its members are ageing with it. The average adult age in 1973 was about 27. By 1994 that was up to over 40 with two members now officially retired. Mortality, which didn't get a look-in in the early years, is making its presence felt. More creaking and groaning, more being careful what we indulge in and how often. Some people have taken to jogging. Tobacco smoking has become very much a minority activity – a vast change from the early years of the community when each weekly meeting involved baccy, papers and matches being tossed round the room, a blue fug settling at eye level. So we all want to stay alive, to be well, to thrive and be active into our old age. And yet, we're going to die. Big problem. So with this awareness, a proposal was put to the group a few years back that we acknowledge this fact.

What had begun to worry some folk was that they would die and be carted off to the local kirk for burial on a religious site that at best meant nothing to them, or at worst, was anathema. The option of being cremated would mean a 50 mile drive to Carlisle – a distant city in another country! Surely we could come up with something better? Two main proposals were put forward. One, that we find a place on our land for our own burial site, and two, that we each answer a series of questions about what we would like to see happen on the event of our death and place a copy in a sealed envelope in the office. Needless to say, the discussions leading up to these proposals were not at all gloomy; rather the reverse as we pitched over into hilarity. How else could we approach the theory of our own demise, especially when sandwiched between discussions about dog shit on the front lawn and the need to buy a new chainsaw?

> ## How else could we approach the theory of our own demise, especially when sandwiched between discussions about dog shit on the front lawn and the need to buy a new chainsaw?

Having decided to have a burial ground was one thing, agreeing where it would be was another. Members were asked to go off and look round our 120 acres or so to find a site that appealed to them and was practicable (that is: it wasn't being used already for anything else, was a bit away from the main centre, but had reasonably easy access). Above all, it needed to have a feeling about it that somehow picked it out as special. A few alternatives were suggested and members then asked to go and see for themselves over a fortnight before coming back to a meeting to decide on a site. Such decisions can be a long process where consensus is used, but in the event one site was the clear favourite and soon became the unanimous choice: about a mile from the main house, just off from a fenced field, bordered by some oak trees with other deciduous trees nearby, but not overhanging, so that the sun shone in, and a broad sweep of marshy land to look out over with not a drop of human activity in sight just lots of wildlife and wind ... lovely!

So we'd agreed this, but would the local planning department? In Scotland at least it's relatively straight forward to get approval for being buried in your own back garden without needing to apply for planning permission, but we were going for a multiple occupancy site, which was a bit different. The planning department was helpful, wanting to know if we were going to do it for a business, or just for ourselves? They visited the site to check on its suitability. This meant seeing that there was no nearby watercourse which could get polluted, checking on the previously designated use of the proposed site, making sure there was enough soil to bury people in, and assessing the site for its impact on any neighbours property, to see if they would need direct consultation. Our site had no problems with these criteria, except for the change in land use that would come about, from agricultural to, well, a graveyard. They did ask us, however, to submit our proposal for planning permission, which meant some form filling, money paying, and a bit of a wait.

Eventually approval came through, but with some conditions: that we build a metre high stone wall round the site; that we mark the graveyard on our deeds and that we don't use it as part of a business. We had five years to build the wall before permission would lapse. At the time that sounded like ages, but time hurries along and it was a while before we got started on the job. By doing the odd half day through one winter, and then by incorporating the work into our thrice yearly Maintenance Weeks, where visitors come to help us, the wall was built, finished in the spring of 1996. And a beautiful co-operative dyke it is too, about 15 metres by 10 with nicely rounded corners and a slot awaiting a gate wide enough to carry someone in with ease. And that's as far as we've got with that. We've planted some more pretty trees nearby, but done little as yet to clear the bracken which grows up each year. We've not talked about whether we want to cultivate the site more, or what limits we might put on people's wishes as to how they are remembered. Would we let someone plant a tree on their grave which might grow to dominate the site?

This leads nicely into the second section of our approach to dying; the completion of a burial plan.

This leads nicely into the second section of our approach to dying; the completion of a burial plan. As a community we have no particular overall religious or political philosophy. Indeed, most people are irreligious, some to the extent of not caring what happens to them when they die, because they'll be dead! So not everybody has lodged a plan in the office. And of those who did, we don't know what they say, as they are private documents, to be opened in the event of ... We don't even know how many people want to be buried here. Some people want to be cremated. Some want to be buried up at the kirk. Some don't want to make the choice of facing up to death in this way.

The one metre high boundary wall going up around Laurieston Hall Community's burial ground.

The questionnaire we created asked people a mixture of things: do you want to be buried here? If so, in what way – in a coffin? In a shroud? Do you want to lie in any particular directon? Would you like to be curled up? What sort of funeral do you want? Do you want any particular music, activities, etc? How would you like your grave marked, if at all? Who would you like to be informed of your death?

and above anything you might have stipulated in a will? And whilst some of us have shared some of what we've written, most of us don't really know what's there in those envelopes. In fact, it's been a while since we wrote them and writing this article makes me think that I should bring up the question of renewal or reconsideration of our wishes. Of course, anybody can change their requests at any time, but, like a lot of things in community, it tends to get overlooked unless there is an issue to focus on, like the first death here, which hasn't happened yet and will be a huge shock.

We are as yet untested in our theories. We have people here who say they are willing and able to lay someone out. We have made enquiries as to who we have to inform on someone's death – a doctor has to certify. As to how we conduct funerals, it seems to be as vague as "doing it in a manner which will not surpass the normal bounds of public decency". The scope is large; the feelings and emotions will be enormous.

The reaction outside the community to our going about this business has been very favourable. We are admired for facing up to our own demise. Maybe it's easier to do in a group. In some ways it can become a project like, say, fixing the gutters, and, in some ways, we've approached it like that, with meeting slots, committees, costings, etc, etc. Questions have come up as to whether ex-members, members' relatives and even just friends could be buried here. On this we have no clear policy. (As a community we're better at "guidelines" than "rules" and in this instance we'll probably take each case as it comes, though being aware that it's easy to set precedents without realising it.)

What of the future? In a way, that's a funny thing to ask, because it feels like we haven't even started yet. We have the foundations, the possible procedures, the site, but we're not using it, and hooray for that! Once someone is there, we will feel massively different about the place. We may well want to set up care and maintenance of the site. It will become a graveyard instead of being a piece of

Readers may also be interested in The Dead Good Funerals Book by Sue Gill and John Fox and published by Engineers of the Imagination (available from Edge of Time for £10.50 including p&p – see page 224).

land with a wall round it. Whoever walks that way will feel differently. No one will be able to walk by without thinking, even if for a brief moment, of who lies there. Up till now the biggest changes we've made to our surroundings have been by felling or planting trees. This change will be much less obvious, but intensely personal in its effect. So there clearly is a sister article to follow this one at some future date: what funerals have we had and how do we deal with death? I hope I don't have to write it for many a year.

Patrick Upton has lived at Laurieston Hall for many years. He once said that it was important for him to do unexpected things in order to prove that he was not a boring old fart!

POST CA

Saturday, Dear Jane,
There's this mantra that gets repeated about life in communities and it has words in it like friendly and tolerant and supportive and sharing and giving and co-operation and flexible — nice cuddly words like that. But let me tell you that the spirit of the late Jo Stalin is alive and well and living at the latest community Frank and I went to, and I know it's Scotland because a lot of them sound like Rab C. Nesbitt on a very bad day! So we get there late last night (train, bus then a mile up some lane), exhausted, but they'd laid on a meeting and we have to answer loads of questions about why we want to join or start a community and what kind of rules we're going to draw up and whether everyone's money will be held in common and do we know how permaculture works and will we allow private cars and will the childcare be shared and will we allow drugs and are we prepared to take on damaged teenagers? And Frank tried to go to the loo at one point but got marched back in by some guy who said that it was important not to interrupt the flow. So we snuck out this morning and we're in some cafe in the village waiting for the bus but ... wait ... here come three of them now, plus a dog! Call the police if I don't turn up to work on Monday!
                                        Love, Emily

A lone piper plays outside Scotland's first public convenience at Lochenva.
Picturesque Lochenva — twinned with Novosibirsk.

r.u.luddite@ commune.uk

ZOE SEWELL

Zoe spent a summer cycling from commune to commune and

pedalling the new technology to communards.

This is what they made of it.

During the Summer of 1996 I was lucky enough to benefit from the hospitality of a number of intentional communities around the country under the pretext of serious academic research. I'd like to take the opportunity to thank all those residents who participated in the workshops and took the time to answer questionnaires. As promised, here are the results.

Okay, so we're all familiar with the Internet then. Everyone knows their URLs from their FTPs and HTTPs and is happily surfing away, part of our brave new world of instant access information, chatting away in Realtime with their new virtual buddies across the globe ... or so we are told. The truth is that although the majority of people have heard of the Net, only a tiny minority of them have actually encountered cyberspace first hand, let alone got to grips with this new, and sometimes daunting, environment. This research focused on how the Internet could be used to facilitate communication between intentional communities, but as it would be unfair to ask the opinion of something such few people had any experience of, the researcher (ie, me!) had to get off her butt and take the technology to the people. So armed with a laptop, modem and yards of cable I went out to

Welcome to the Findhorn Bay Community!

We are an international community and developing a eco-village of about 350 people living, studying and working together in the northeast of Scotland. The community was founded in 1962 by Eileen Caddy, Peter Caddy and Dorothy Maclean in a caravan park a mile from the seaside village of Findhorn. First known for our work with plants and nature, we have since become a centre for spiritual and holistic education as well.

While we have no formal doctrine or creed, we honour and recognise all the major world religions, believing that there are many paths to God. Our focus is on listening to bring spiritual principles into our daily lives through our work, the way we relate to each other, and how we express our caring and concern for the Earth.

Educational Centre

The Findhorn Foundation runs an educational centre and offers a wide variety of courses in such fields as personal and spiritual growth, conflict resolution, gardening, meditation, leadership, community living, and the arts.

The Findhorn Foundation Home Page

introduce the Net to the fine body of people that make up the intentional communities of the UK.

I ran a workshop introducing the Internet and its facilities – electronic mail (e-mail), newsgroups and the World Wide Web (www – the glossy, graphic face of the Internet). Many workshop participants were surprised to see that the net already contains a lot of information about intentional communities. This is mainly US stuff, but a growing number of UK communities are making their debut in cyberspace. The potential does exist for an electronic Communes Network, but there are many things to be taken into consideration before that can become a reality. I prepared a questionnaire to ask community residents what they thought about inter-communal communication in general and electronic communication in particular. I was blessed with intelligent and thoughtful comments (in the main!) and in total the results appear to show a positive desire to maintain contact. What must be borne in mind, however, is that this was by no means comprehensive research and for every community who wants to stay in touch there could be three that want nothing to do with anyone!

The vast majority of questionnaire respondents were already in contact with other communities, mainly through visits, telephone or newsletters. Gatherings such as the annual Inter-Communal Volleyball Tournament were mentioned, as well as other 'informal' gatherings and festivals. Other networks such as Radical Routes as well as **Diggers and Dreamers**, and also environmental, religious and local networks featured, depending on the philosophy of the community. When asked about what benefits inter-communal communication held for them, the majority of respondents mentioned mutual support and the exchange of information and experience:

● Sharing resources/ideas and lessons/energy and inspiration

● Exchange of information (technical advice etc) learning lessons from others' experience

● I think it's good communicating to find out what other people are doing how they're doing it and feeling the support of other communities

● General support. "Just good to meet like-minds." Specific support. "Somebody has usually done it before." Personal support.

● Seeing how each community is different, the issues they have, and how they deal with them.

Others saw the benefit as more of a form of camaraderie:

● It brings together many voices into one. The louder one voice the better it will be heard

● Whittling away at the isolation of being the only people going through this*!?*

● Sharing experience, meeting people, having a laugh, feeling part of something bigger, not so isolated

Most workshop participants were interested in the e-mail facility as a possibility for quick, cheap communication. During the research for the project it was apparent that the usual reason for the lack of communication was a lack of time and money. More importantly, networks established to maintain links between communities often floundered because of the financial and administrative problems associated with operating. The findings of this research suggested that an electronic network held a number of advantages over the paper-based networks of before, *but* also had drawbacks, greatest of which is access to the technology.

However, perhaps going against the media image of 'back-to-the-land technophobics', many communities do actually have access to computers, either individually owned by a member or used by the community for accounts, business or publicity. A number are used for communicating, for example, four of the **Diggers and Dreamers** editorial group have e-mail addresses and use the facility extensively. For basic e-mail communication, it

---

Residents' opinions of the World Wide Web varied:

"It was okay but not great – early days. It's a lot harder if you have no money, live in tipi valley and have no electricity. [Only public access to] those with money and status!"

"If access [to?] this is restricted (moneywise) as the traditional media is then there will be no alternative to their traditional opinions. The media is based on selling products to the public the www doesn't interest me much if it boils down to the same thing."

Some were rather more ambivalent, although they were aware of the web's potential, some were doubtful as to the usefulness of the information.

"Seems interesting. I haven't yet found info I wanted to solve particular problems."

"I would like to have an access point in a library ... I think it could be a public service. Does not need to be privately owned."

"Potentially useful as a way of distributing information, potentially somewhere to drown in the sea of info!"

"It's always the dullest people/organisations that have most to say ... Seriously, charities/campaigning groups are doing a great job of owning the Web for good causes."

"What are we doing with all the informations, which are 'easier' available? (sic)"

Others were more abrupt:

"Can be great, can be totally useless"

"Complex!"

"Underimpressed"

Opinions about the 'Information Superhighway' and its potential varied enormously, from good:

"Super. Vast. Potentially time consuming. Easy to get lost!"

"It's a long time coming. I've been waiting all my conscious life for some such thing (and much more.)"

"Interested in finding out more. It could be a massive tool for resistance and change in our world."

to bad:

"American rubbish, commercial."

is not necessary to have all the elaborate bells and whistles that computer magazines sing about. The computer itself could be a cheap, second-hand model. Extra considerations involve using a modem (to connect to the telephone network) and an Internet service provider (ISP) such as Compuserve or Demon or any number of local suppliers. All of the Internet magazines in newsagents or in libraries provide lists of ISPs, rating them according to their services and costs.

It does not have to be an expensive business either. Once the initial equipment is set up, the payments will consist of an account with your ISP (monthly

---

"Biased towards people with access and money, everything should be free, too much emphasis on crap mass media trivia and personal information."

to wary:

"Good in the right way, but what about the risk of government spying or terrorists?"

"Has uses, concerned – people can get lost in it, concerned if decreases face to face communication."

"Yes, we have to use it or it will use us. Telly too."

"Suspect 'hyped' is part of my opinion; also I wonder if it becomes something else which excludes the poor etc."

"Yuppie CB [Citizens' Band] – in the wrong hands. Dead good for communities who are trying to improve quality of life."

"Like TV could be good, but will probably become part of Babylon – not everyone can have."

and to plain realistic:

"Aye, if it's all for free – it is information that should be free, fuck this paying money lets just share."

"Expensive and time consuming. Expensive in that you need a computer and a 'phone link. Computers are full of environmentally unfriendly materials."

"We'd have some of us in the driving seat, with others lying in front of the information bulldozers."

"Not interested. I think a lot of potential is in it but reality is, it's not really used."

"Superhighway, more like urban motorway at 5.30 on Friday afternoon."

"Something I personally won't use as I don't know about it. Sounds like it has amazing potential for linking communities and others across the planet. A valuable resource if you've got the time and money."

"More a footpath than a highway at the moment – much hyped, but useful."

"Frustrating, brilliant, crap, excellent, waste of time, invaluable – contrary – I can't decide whether it's good or bad."

"Expensive to link into and paying the phone bill could be a nightmare – but I'd love to have access to that much information; danger of losing garden time."

usually between £6 – £15) and, of course, your telephone bill. The important thing to remember is that the calls you make are all at the *local* rate which can be less than 1p per minute depending on the time of day. When it comes to sending or receiving e-mail, the time you spend on the phone can be literally seconds as the actually reading and writing takes place 'offline' (ie you only connect when you're ready to send the final message).

The biggest 'like' of e-mail was to do with speed and one of the main barriers to inter-communal communication was said to be lack of time. This suggests that e-mail could well be an efficient method of increasing inter-communal contact. Indeed, this was the facility which most interested workshop participants. Problems encountered by the snail-mail *Communes Network* were to do with administrative costs in time and energy as well as financial.

There is a good possibility that as the costs of the technology decreases, communication between communities in this way could increase. Whether or not an 'electronic Communes Network' could evolve depends on the interest level of the communities. This of course is not as easy to predict!

> **e-mail could well be an efficient method of increasing inter-communal contact**

The other facilities such as newsgroups and the wwwdid not appear as relevant to the workshop participants, although the idea of their individual communities having their own websites interested them. When I embarked upon the research of intentional communities on the www, I found that the Fellowship for Intentional Community in the US (who produce the **Communities Directory**) had a website and were in the process of asking some of their listed communities if they would like to be listed on the website. Eight months later there were over 150 individual communities listed; overwhelmingly US but some international and two UK (one of whom I had not encountered before).

al and two UK (one of whom I had not encountered before).

Getting it together

Apart from time, the major barrier to communication was financial. With a couple of notable exceptions, intentional communities are not wealthy. Their disposable income is usually concentrated on maintaining the communal area – the house and land. Although individuals within the communities may have a desire for a computer and in many cases may

The Co-Construction web site put together by Zoe herself

already own one, the purchase of equipment for the community as a whole would have to be agreed by the community. As these decisions are usually arrived at in communal meetings, there could be other expenditure which could be considered more pressing by other members. Opposing members may not see any benefit to the community in the ownership of a computer, especially if they feel the technology is 'unsound' or they personally have no interest in using one. It is not the case of deciding to buy or not to buy (difficult enough for individuals and family groups), but of arriving at a decision which satisfies the whole community which may involve anywhere up to 100 people.

This unique situation illustrates the importance of available understandable information for non-computer literate members which can be presented at meetings. Information based on jargon-free pros and cons relevant to the use of the computer and not the computer itself. Of course, once a decision has been made the more technical decisions regarding specifications would then have be addressed, again these decisions could involve more than one individual if finance was an issue. Perhaps the best solu-

or group. Evidently, for those communities without a computer, the process is not a simple one and could take a long time. One of the benefits stressed by respondents concerning inter-communal communication was the sharing of information and experience. Almost symbolically then, the use of communication between those communities who already own a computer and those who are looking to buy one could assist the decision-making process for the latter.

Benefits of Electronic Communication.

Intentional communities have a lot of requests for further information about their lifestyle and have to answer frequently asked questions which can become a tedious and expensive business. When it comes to 'outsiders', who may have an interest in community lifestyles, the Internet could provide some advantages. A web site covering the issues surrounding a community can be a way of distributing information in a form which requires little manual effort. Redfield Community's web site was online by the July 22 1996 and they had received genuine visitor inquiries by September 1. As Redfield is presently looking for new members to join their community, using the web as a means of advertising their existence has been a success. The downside of this method of publicity is that the volume of inquiry-related traffic could rise dramatically. Casually interested individuals could request information for which they perhaps wouldn't bother if there were postage costs involved.

A page from the Redfield Community web site

An interesting point arising from the questionnaire results was the different choices made

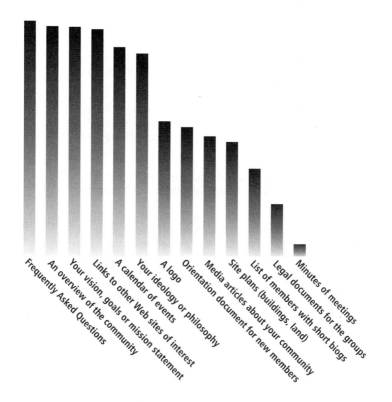

An interesting point arising from the questionnaire results was the different choices made by
members of the same community for what they would
like to see in a newsletter or on a web site. This reflects
the differences that would have to be reconciled when
considering the design of a web site for a collective
but heterogeneous group of people. The results
(see above) show a willingness to share general information, but a wariness of making internal information
public knowledge, for example, for example there
was little support for making the minutes of meetings public.

**What
communards
would like to
see on their
web site**

multi-billion dollar interests to protect, who could easily use their corporate muscle to influence the evolution of this baby; there are big and little commercial actors who see the net as solely another advertising medium and there are millions of individuals for whom the Internet is no more than another way to watch a box.

So a focus on electronic communication as the solution to communication problems would be foolish. A number of people echoed these feelings:

- Has uses, concerned – people can get lost in it, concerned if decreases face-to-face communication

- Prefer face-to-face communication – eg at Radical Routes quarterly gatherings – we have to make time to be together. Computers have a place, but shouldn't be central to our dealings.

- I suspect communicating with people elsewhere in the world could be a very convenient escape from keeping on trying with the people I'm actually living with – and for that reason I am rather wary of it all.

The Internet is here, it is only one more tool in our evolution. Its effect could be positive (as the axe was for human survival) or it could be negative (as the axe was for human carnage). As any communard would agree – *we* decide.

Zoe Sewell is moving from the virtual community into the real thing. After two years of studying intentional communities, she's embarking on co-operative living and learning first hand. She hopes to continue pressing home the message of electronic communication and can be contacted at zsewell@compuserve.com

---

From Autumn 1997
Diggers and Dreamers is on the
WORLD WIDE WEB
http://www.gaia.org/diggers-dreamers

POST CA

Sunday, Dear Jane,

Might take my mind off things to scribble this card to you ... I've fled upstairs to the Visitors' Room — Frank and I are at this community in Norfolk or Suffolk or somewhere like that — it's very flat — and I just got caught up in this really scary row between two of the mums that seem to have about 16 kids between them (I exaggerate). One of the kids grabbed a Power Ranger (I thought these places were right on!) off another kid, and the second kid belted the first kid, and the first kid's mum asked the second kid's mum if she was going to let her kid get away with that, and the second kid's mum said the first kid had to learn not to grab, and the first kid's mum said the second kid had never learned to share (implying that she knew whose fault that was!) and by this time both the kids were happily chasing each other around the garden but the mums were looking angry and pretty sniffy and I got really terrified one of them might ask me what I thought, so here I am writing to you while Frank's checking the timetable to see if there's an earlier train ...

Love, Emily

Madonna and Child (photo: K Herod)
The Shrine of Our Lady of Walsingham

Book Review

Chris Coates (a member of People in Common Community) reviews:
The Future will be Green
by **The Venerable Anelog and Brother Sebastien**

ISBN: 0 9529120 0 7
Positive Press, 1997 ● 288pp paperback ● £14

Anelog and Sebastien, along with another brother Hereward, form the monastic core of the Graigian Society. Self-styled green monks (See entry in Directory Section) they follow a philosophy drawn heavily from Jung, Gurdjieff and the green movement. Their book, illustrated with many black and white line drawings by Hereward, is less of a book and more a collection of essays going back some 20 years, covering the whole range of Graigian ideas from their view of history, through sexuality, spirituality, criminality, devolution and cleaning up the countryside. Woven in amongst all this is a story of the birth of the green movement on a Welsh mountainside in 1965 and the setting up of the Graigian Society in 1983.

As I read it, the book struck me as strangely out of time. Partly the whole thing has a flavour of early 20th century utopian writing of the likes of Eric Gill, and partly the lack of any reference to other work that has gone on based on the ideas of Jung and Gurdjieff. Not being a Jungian psychologist I have no idea if the Graigians' ideas on sexuality or dreams make any sense at all, but the use of strange terms and symbols makes reading the whole chapter a feat in itself – let alone understanding it. Some of the writing seems dated (which if it was written up to 20

years ago is not really a suprise), other bits seem just plain eccentric – shades of Edith Sitwell. I can imagine that they would not have been out of place as early settlers in some of the new garden cities – they claim to be 20 years ahead of their times, but in many ways they seem 60 years out of time.

All that aside it is a wonderful chronicle of some of the more colourful characters that make up the green movement and the strange pot-pourri of ideas that goes under the banner of the New Age.

Book Review

Dave Hodgson (a member of Old Hall Community) reviews:
Shared Visions, Shared Lives by **Bill Metcalf**

ISBN: 1 899171 01 0 ● Findhorn Press, 1996 ● 192pp paperback ● £7.95 (available from "Edge of Time Ltd" for £8.95 including p&p, see page 224)

A valuable book for any person wishing to understand more about the communal way of living. Fifteen people who have lived in communities for a large part of their lives, thirty years or more, tell about their personal histories, their spiritual development, their political and social awakening, through the wisdom of experience. The selection of essays has been carefully choreographed by the author to cover such diverse communal activities as leadership, commitment, accessibility, relationship, ritual, conflict resolution, utopian quest and gender roles.

The communards whose stories are told here come from all corners of the world. There are accounts of communities in Japan, Mexico, India, New Zealand, Brazil, as well as the USA and Europe. The author himself has lived for many years in communities and has personally visited most of the places to which this book refers. His lifetime commitment to the academic study of community and its changing role in the new world order provides him with the understanding and wisdom to undertake such a task as this. The lives of the contributors provide the diversity needed to take the reader on an emotional journey of communal living around the globe.

This book is a good read and a must for all who are interested in this lifestyle. I will leave you with a few words from one contributor, Rachel Summerton, who's sentiment sums up my own personal experiences of communal living.

"I had nothing materially when I came, but now I have the things that really count. If I had wanted riches, I'd have remained in outer society. It's the intangibles which one can't buy that matter: friendship, care, support, spirituality, peace and vision. I earned these things by working together with others and by trying a new communal lifestyle – giving up the old for the new. Communal living is my sanity and my health. No one promised it would be easy! Walking a new way through the briars and thistles of communalism is much more difficult than following a well worn path. I can, however, stop and smell the roses."

Go out and buy this book.

Confessions of a Serial Communard

MIKE FROM REDFIELD

From Glenfield to Redfield in 27 years

In 1970 I ran away to my first commune, only to find that in the blessed groves of the Utopian dream irony still held sway.

This was a shock. Youth has an immodest belief in its own power and like no generation before (or since) we were convinced we could create a parallel universe, a suspension of normal rules, a new social cosmology immune from the past. So as the likelihood of revolution waned after the dizzy heights of Paris '68 some of us picked up the ball and wandered off to start our own game.

Both the hopeful and the hopeless had gathered at Glenfield (an old farm near Sydney, Australia) in the belief that an old Quaker called Jim would bestow that part of his property on them rather than his heirs, who were watching from the other side of the fence. Despite these uncertain beginnings, a pattern repeated many times since, Glenfield was to go on for over twenty years.

'Sex, Drugs and Rock'n'Roll' seemed a frivolous description even then of a movement that had its roots as much in political activism as the quakings of youth. But it does make a neat developmental index.

Sex had only just been discovered and wasn't aware of the degree of political correction it was to incur. And I was never convinced that the new paradigm could be entered via the products of radical chemistry. They very quickly turned into mass-produced comestibles and pyramid-selling schemes that smacked too much of the old ways. Rock'n'roll seemed to be weighed down by similar contradictions – and still is.

Australian communities were, generally, to take the form of homesteading groups scattered over a few dozen acres. Glenfield was closer to the British model – a communal group in a big old house with not the faintest idea of how it was going to support itself. Other elements of this model already in place included a small milking herd, organic vegetable garden, tennis court and grand piano.

A whiff of irony was already mixing with the compost.

A fierce intolerance of anything organisational meant that there was a completely opaque unofficial structure revolving round one older and shrewder member who was only too happy to oblige! In some later groups such structural vacuums, when added to the tendency of events to assume an exaggerated importance in communities, became fertile ground for some grotesque projections. The driving intensities of the hive/cult where all energy is drawn to a bloated manipulator at the centre of the infestation. So! If the cap fits ...

Yet another vulnerability was present at Glenfield. There was a tacit agreement not to let the dream be threatened by close scrutiny. Issues were shelved. Thus we were condemned to approaching everything obliquely; a mental mode akin to conventional ideas of madness which wasn't helped by some of us being perilously close to this concept already. One member lived in what had been the outside toilet, where he presumably slept standing up. Another, preferred eye-contact marathons to conversations and would lock pupils with the unwary ... for distressing lengths of time. We felt we had to indulge

him in case he was onto something deep and meaningful rather than simply having a kangaroo loose
in the top paddock.

We were exquisitely sensitive to anything tainted
by old process. Nothing could be 'caused' – it
could only 'happen'. This made joining difficult.
One day you weren't there the next day you were,
or vice versa. My vice-versa came on a day when
the gods of irony were smiling broadly. My lack of
interest in alternative chemistry was rewarded
when a group of us were thrown out – accused of
taking the wrong drugs.

Back in Britain in the early eighties I began to
think of gentling myself back into the dream after
a stint in the other reality. Communities were taking on a Butlinesque quality and were offering an
endless list of worthy experiences.

So I chose my event, travelled overnight, walked the
last twelve miles and collapsed at the door, where
the redcoats found me and told me it was cancelled.

From earliest days communities found themselves
awash with visitors but very few of these were
seriously interested in joining, so the shrewder
groups realised what the market was and created
suitable packages to cater for these 'seekers after
smooth things'.

But other groups seemed to collude in their visitors' delusion that there were no bills to pay in Utopia.
Most groups have trouble recycling the moun-
tainous piles of letters from American post-graduates
wanting free passage through. What is needed is a
more liquid form of foreign exchange.

If your alternative reality is going to be housed in
a big house in the country with surrounding acreage,
it will need financing. A consideration that didn't
seem to bother founding groups all that much.

Unlike American communities with their ham-
mock, shoe and nut-butter plants, British com-

munards didn't seem keen on the messy business of manufacturing. Hence the drift into the service sector. There was even a reluctance to name the phenomenon for what it was. Except perhaps at Lower Shaw Farm, where they advertised in the ordinary holiday press.

Has the dream been compromised by the aggressive pursuit of market share and the fact that you can't buy your alternative experiences with alternative money?

Certainly, the media and academia still find communities fascinating. You can't walk round a corner at Redfield without falling over a journalist or someone writing a thesis about 'Communes as the model for colonies on Mars'.

Having come to rest at Redfield irony demands that it mirror my beginnings in communities. Glenfield to Redfield – even the words are similar and the tennis court and grand piano have followed me. But there is one crucial difference. At Redfield the Captain didn't shoot himself in the front room, he was turfed out by the RAF during the war[1].

Now as the dial on my wireless finds its way to Radio 2 I enjoy beating my fellow members over the head with my twenty-seven year perspective. But a recent spate of new young members means that even though I'm getting older 'our' average age is going down. This is only possible in the paradoxical 'New Age' physics of communities.

In similar vein someone recently showed me a book which maintained that no communities existed in Australia before 1972. This is disturbing as I was sure that it all really happened. But although the Gods of Irony continue to sink their teeth into my backside in such ways, I was recently assured that it remains wrinkle-free.

[1] Both Glenfield and Redfield had been occupied by army captains in their earlier incarnations. Glenfield's captain had committed suicide at the end of the nineteenth century while Captain Lambton of Redfield had to leave suddenly when his house was requisitioned by the Air Ministry in 1942.

Mike has been a member of three communities and spent considerable time in several others in the period since 1970. He is currently a member of Redfield Community where he has lived since 1990. His principal interest is community life itself.

Do we have Consensus

SARAH BUNKER

Believe it or not, consensus decision-making is one of the things

that attracts some people to communal living ... but, Bunk asks,

"does it all have to end in magnolia walls?"

A classic anecdote is often given by non- or ex-communards as to why they don't live in a commune: "They spend hours and hours deciding the colour of the front door", they say, and one has visions of a smokey parlour filled with hippies pontificating on the political significance of colour schemes. To some extent, I thought this was an apocryphal tale ... but then it happened to us.

It took us literally months to decide on the new colour of the 'green' room; which turned out to be yellow. Why did it take so long to come to this decision? On the surface, it seemed to be difficult because colour is so subjective, and the green room is a communal room which also serves as space hired to outside groups. But this whole episode left the older members – who had dealt with insolvency, bailiffs, repossessions and setting up the present trust and co-op – a little bemused. Was it a case of 'pointed' versus 'smooth' decisions? Perhaps during the insolvency, when big decisions involving large sums of money, court action and homelessness were dealt with on a day-to-day basis, the process was very 'pointed'; everyone's attention was focused on a narrow band of possibilities and survival depended on swift, concerted action. In contrast, the green room could be painted any old colour and no-one would lose their life savings or have to move out; a smooth arc of possibilities stretched from here to the horizon, with no landmarks at all.

This experience got me thinking about the decision process, which is obviously a concern for anyone who attempts to live communally (except for those who hand over decision-making to a leader).

As a community, Beech Hill tries to use consensus to arrive at decisions, but is it best? (And being above all a pragmatic place, we have voting followed by mediation followed by arbitration as back-up, none of which we have had to use so far.)

Consensus is really the sacred cow of decision-making; is it all that it is cracked up to be? Bill Mollison, in **Permaculture** says:

"Consensus, in particular, is an endless and pointless affair, with coercion of the often silent or incoherent abstainer by a vociferous minority. Thus decisions reached by boards, parliaments, and consensus groups either oppress some individuals (votes) or are vetoed by dissenters. In either case we have tyranny of a majority or tyranny of a minority, and a great deal of frustration and wasted time."

This may be the case if lip-service alone is paid to the process, but we have found consensus very effective. How does it work? Once a proposal or topic is put forward, there usually follows an exchange of opinions, agreement or counter proposals. As many relevant reasons for agreement or disagreement as possible are encouraged; in this way the 'bones' of the matter are approached (which may not be obvious at first). It is at this stage that it may become apparent that there is not enough basic information to make a decision. Lack of information can lead to frustrating spirals of speculation and it's best to stop discussing the issue until the information can be brought back to the group.

During the discussion, anyone may ask someone who is remaining silent what their views are. There are many reasons why someone may be remaining silent; lack of interest, some volcanic opinion simmering below the surface, lack of understanding of the topic, or even what the problem is, lack of confidence or downright intimidation . Likewise, anyone may call for a 'round' in which everyone's opinions are heard. These two techniques avoid losing valuable input and also prevent people from remaining silent and claiming later that they didn't have a chance to speak.

This process won't work if the participants are not looking for a workable solution; if people want to sabotage the process, there is ample room to do so. People need to enter into it with the right attitude and they have to speak their minds. So the process won't work if there are already deep divisions and factions who are not willing to meet each other.

Cartoon by
Massimo

SO IT'S AGREED...

WE **WON'T** DECIDE THE COLOUR OF THE WALLS

BY CONSENSUS

Probably the most important aspect of attitude to go into a consensus meeting with is that of 'give and take'. We all know that we aren't going to get what we want every time, but most of the time (because we chose to live together and share some ethics), we will. You have to use your own judgement as to when to stand up and when to back down, and how to do that only comes with sharing your life with other people in a workable way. It may be that this dynamic equilibrium is the heart of consensus.

As the discussion progresses, usually some suggestion will win general approval. This may happen when new ideas have stopped coming forward and one person puts forward a proposal, which is either accepted or modified to take account of concerns which have been brought up.

Sometimes there appears to be general approval and then a concern will turn the whole argument on its head. At other times a dissenter may say that they don't entirely agree with the decision, but will go along with it because they don't consider it worth fighting over. Sometimes a decision cannot be reached at all, in which case the whole discussion is deferred to another meeting. In the intervening period another process occurs as the topic is chewed over informally and a completely different view may come to light in the next session.

Decisions take longer the more contentious, irreversable and subjective the issue; some of our lengthier discussions are on such topics as what to do about dog shit, issues of work input and acceptance of new members. Sometimes consensus works very quickly, and it certainly becomes easier the more you get to know your fellow communards.

Although we meet once a week, for about two and a half hours, we don't bring every little decision to the Co-op meeting. Sub-groups make decisions on maintenance, gardens, courses and admin and individuals and informal groups are constantly making day-to-day decisions as well. We also have

At Beech Hill Community they found it so difficult to decide what colour to paint the walls that they moved all the furniture out on to the lawn instead!

a 'brownie' system in which ideas are circulated in old manilla envelopes (hence the name) for comment by everyone; a process that saves valuable meeting time since opinions have already been aired. The weekly meeting relates more to subjects which affect our overall aims; money, space, time, legal matters, people, creative ideas, and ethical stance.

So what went wrong with our decision process when we tried to choose a colour for the green room? Starhawk, when discussing consensus in her book **Truth or Dare** notes a few situations when it's best to avoid using it – one of these is if the issue is trivial: "Remember, consensus is a thinking process – when there is nothing to think about, flip a coin." She also recommends flipping a coin if the choice to be made is between two dreadful options, for example if the group has to choose between being shot or being hanged.

Another time when it would be prudent to give consensus a miss is in an emergency – "When they can see the whites of your eyes." In this case, a temporary leader may be the best way to go.

Perhaps we are able to relax into consensus because we know that we have the conventional backup of voting if we need it. Perhaps it would be a lot heavier if our rules only allowed for consensus – maybe then we would suffer more tyranny.

And as for the colour of walls ... is it possibe to tell the decision making process of a commune by looking at the walls? Does the swing from every-wall-a-different-primary- colour of the 70s to magnolia of the 80s tell us something? Yes, at Beech Hill we have a few magnolia walls, but a peek into someone's bedroom would assure you that colour schemes with attitude are not a thing of the past.

Sarah Bunker is a long-term member of Beech Hill Community. Her room has orange walls.

POST C

Dear Jane,

Do you remember that course we did at university about the Chinese Cultural Revolution and how the Maoists sat round once a day and criticised each other so they could become better people? I wonder if it works ...? Frank and I went to another community on the weekend (sorry about your birthday – we'll make it next year!), and guess what – they still do that! Every evening, an hour before supper, everybody gathers in a large room with cushions and they sit in a circle and somebody starts in: "Fred, I have to say, with all due respect, that the back stairs were covered in sheep shit this morning (what does that mean!?)." Then Fred says, "I'm really sorry about that, and I'll try to keep the sheep in my room (what does that mean!?), but you know, Carla, the surfaces in the kitchen were pretty crummy at lunchtime." And then Carla says she'll try to do better but attacks Alice and Alice apologises but has a go at Tom, and then they troop into dinner and it's all very quiet. I tried it out on Frank tonight and he's stormed off to the pub.

Hmmm ...

Love, Emily

Sheep at play on the Mountainside (photo: Larry Lamluva) The Merioneth Mountain Sheep is well known for its especially furry fleece and extreme friendliness towards human beings.

Pecking at the Group Process

ANDY WOOD

Community Building (CB) is a group dynamics process and communications technique created by M Scott Peck and described in his book **The Different Drum**. *In Diggers and Dreamers 94/95 Laurence Brightbart explained what it was all about, and here Andy Wood investigates the practical use of such techniques in intentional communities.*

From his experience as a psychiatrist and group therapist, Peck observed that groups which related very well together go through three stages prior to reaching a desired state of relating. This desired state he calls 'genuine' or 'true community'.

Peck's method of Community Building helps a group experience going through these three stages – called 'pseudo-community', 'chaos' and 'emptiness' – and aims towards reaching 'true community'. There is no guarantee that a group will get there of course, and some that do, slip out of it again. As Laurence says in his article, the main characteristic of a group experienced at CB is its ability to notice that something has gone out of balance and act to correct it.

Community Building in Britain (CBiB) formed in 1990 as an organisation to host and facilitate two or three day workshops which provide an opportunity for groups of people to learn these skills. They define community as:

> "a group ... who, regardless of the diversity of their personal backgrounds or ideology, age, race, gender, sexuality or politics, have been able to accept, transcend and celebrate their differences. This enables them to communicate openly, to bridge difficulties with integrity, and to work and play together in a generous and rewarding way ... The process supports individuals in being who they are and in reaching out to others being who they are, through communication grounded in acceptance of self and other."

Whilst a lot of emphasis in Britain has gone into running publicly open workshops to which participants come together purely for the Community Building experience, in the States the process has been used amongst organisations as a group dynamics tool. I don't know how successful that's been, but I've often felt it should be put to such uses here. And I've got especially excited about its possible usefulness to communal groups. So I've developed a little pet hypothesis which goes: groups who want to create a community to live in together will benefit from Community Building together ... if you get my meaning.

I live in a housing co-operative that, frankly, isn't very mature at handling the group process. It has survived however for nearly twenty years, fluctuating mostly between 'pseudo-community' and 'chaos'; with occasional, fleeting experiences of 'true community' after a good party or workday; or from closing ranks in response to outside pressures. But survive is all it's done. It hasn't matured into a group that is emotionally safe, inclusive or nurturing for its members. Neither is it respectful of differences and able to fight gracefully with love and compassion for our differences. It also shies away from differences in its housing allocations practice, despite the equal opportunities policy.

Conflicts have been buried, scapegoats found. People's stuff and community issues litter our history unresolved. And hurts fester. Rumour even has it that a member many years ago co-wrote a manual about better meetings using ours as her negative model. It was called **Co-operative and Community Group Dynamics ... or Your Meetings Needn't Be so Appalling.**

I've often fantasised about our group partaking of a Community Building workshop. Encouragingly there has been some interest shown in it recently. But it's hard to imagine more than just a few people willing to spend two days sat in a circle together. Having come together with several different groups of people intent on forming a community, with only one actually doing so, I've also felt a Community Building workshop would be a great way to start such a group off. Anyway, I decided to investigate further afield. What existing or forming communities have used the Community Building process, and with what results?

it's hard to imagine more than just a few people willing to spend two days sat in a circle together

Braziers in Oxfordshire, was the first of three groups I contacted. I spoke to George, one of three people there who admired the books of M Scott Peck before they knew of CBiB. These three residents, accompanied by two Friends of Braziers (participants that don't live there) investigated by attending a public workshop. They returned full of enthusiasm for the process and keen to introduce the method into the community. But they met with resistance.

Braziers is one of the longest surviving communities in Britain; one of a few that set up shortly after the Second World War. The social climate from which its now ageing founder members set out to experiment with "new ways of working and living together" was very different from the one most of us dug and dreamt from. And they developed their own methods for "self-counselling and governance" guided by newly emerging ideas in the sociology and psychology of their day. Newer members, from a different generation, find that these methods don't work so well today. It has been a struggle to convince the elders that maybe some alternative methods of communicating and group work should be investigated. The resistance is relenting, but older members have tended to observe rather than participate in the new process, says George.

A Braziers CBiB event was held last year. It was a public workshop and most participants were not connected with Braziers. Three of the eight residents attended, plus a couple of Friends of Braziers. Other residents saw it only as an event at, rather than for, the community. George explained that since then they have introduced CB techniques into meetings, sometimes with good effect, and at other times not. And in any case it was, he said, one of several different group relating methods they were beginning to experiment with.

So not a lot to go on there. George, however, still felt optimistic about the benefits of CB, once you could convince the rest of the group to try it. If a CB workshop is held at a community, but is not exclusively for the community, I can't see how it could have much benefit to the community. It could even result in unhelpful consequences, for both the community and the workshop. Indeed my next contact bore this out.

Was Community Building appropriate for 'living together' type communities, I asked Alex at Monkton Wyld?

"No way!" Her instant reaction was a rather startling and somewhat unexpected rebuttal of my hypothesis. A little deflated but not defeated, I asked her to explain. Her first experience of Community Building was attending a two day Community Building workshop at the now defunct Sharpham North Buddhist community in Devon. She was bemused, she said, and I guess quite a little annoyed to discover half way through the event that about half the participants were community members and most of the other half were their friends. It didn't seem to help her or the community.

Despite this, Monkton Wyld did hold their own CB event exclusively for its members. At last, I thought, I'm getting somewhere. CB events are usually facilitated by two people, who 'hold the process' for the group, but intervene only very occasionally. In devising the process, Scott Peck determined that a group needs to be together for at least two days to enable the greatest opportunity of achieving 'true community'. Monkton Wyld's workshop was for a day and a half in the first instance, followed by three half-day events.

The community had, Alex said, a lot of entrenched positions on unresolved conflict and personal differences. There was, therefore, so much "stuff" going on, that the CB process didn't seem able to cope. Day-to-day patterns within the community were not sufficiently challenged by the participants, or through the intervention of the facilitators. So the group did not work through them. There are, in Alex's opinion, better group dynamic processes around which can assist communities. Her recommendation is to find outside facilitators experienced in psychotherapeutic group and individual processes, who also know something about how living communities work.

Given my own community's reluctance – or is it paranoia even – to confront conflict and work with group dynamics, it was refreshing to hear Alex say that willingness to do so is a prerequisite for Monkton Wyld residents these days. I salivated as she explained that the community meets every morning for about 20 minutes. This is mostly to sort out the business of running their visitor centre, but it is also a space to deal with feelings and all that mucky group process stuff. And everyone is expected to attend. In addition to this they have fortnightly contact meetings. These are for sharing and processing emotions. They might take a variety of forms, like dancing or talking, for example. Then they have day long reviews of life in the community for which they have outside facilitators, which take place quarterly.

I know Monkton Wyld is very different from my housing co-op. Here we all have our own seperate houses and we don't run a business together. But one monthly meeting, at which business always dominates and conflicts get pushed firmly under the carpet (and occassionally but regularly fester up and disrupt proceedings) is never enough. At least Alex agrees with me that a community has to pay as much – if not more – attention to the maintenance of the people as the property. As for CB, she said it was an "impossible" process for groups living and working together.

I was scrambling around now to save my hypothesis from the dustbin. Did she think that CB could be useful in some instances? I suggested that maybe a new group setting up a community would benefit from starting their creative process with a CB workshop. Maybe an exclusive workshop for those coming together would focus the forming, norming, storming phase of group process. From a place of 'true community' such a group could undertake the task of visualising and agreeing principles and values; later on, it could set goals and plan. Well yes, thought Alex, that might be an appropriate use of CB. So I called John, a bloke I had met at a men's weekend where we had discovered a mutual interest in Community Building and communal living. Had his group used the Community Building process from the outset?

Cony Garth Farm existed as a communal household of seven adults and five children for just eight months, John told me. Yes they had had ten consecutive weeks of a two hour CB facilitated workshop to which all of them committed themselves. Coming together out of a larger group who had abandoned communal aspirations, this group began to live in the farm before the CB process was complete. The result was it merely clarified underlying differences between them, and their unwillingness to "do what it takes" to overcome those differences to create community, said John.

Well perhaps that was a good thing. It enabled the group to get clear that they weren't right for each other. In some senses this suggests the CB process was successful. But in another way it failed. As John pointed out, the process did not enable those individuals to let go of whatever was necessary in order to create community with each other. And that is what the CB process sets out to do.

Many would-be communal groups must surely come together because they feel they have enough values and principles in common and like each other enough, and founder on the differences that emerge in the process of forming. It doesn't need CB to bring these out although it could enable it to happen more quickly and without loss of good will. But the potential benefit of CB to such a would-be communal group is that it should allow them to fight gracefully and ultimately transcend such differences.

John's assessment concurred with my revised hypothesis, that for CB to benefit communal groups it needs to be introduced at the very start. Even then, John adds, each individual must be prepared to "do what it takes". And in his experience, the others were not.

In conclusion, the evidence so far suggests that other group dynamic methods suit communities just as well if not better. Maybe, as Alex says, it doesn't work well for groups working and living together. (But I would be interested to hear from other communities who have tried it.) Can it help forming communal groups? I still believe that it can but I've yet to find groups that have tried it. So my pet hypothesis (or is it my 'peck' hypothesis?!) is qualified and as yet unproven.

Andy Wood lives in a housing co-operative and is a member of Community Building in Britain, an organisation inspired by the writing of M Scott Peck. Community Building in Britain can be contacted via:
125 Greenham Road, Newbury, Berkshire RG14 7JE.

POST C

Tuesday, Dear Jane,

God, what I wouldn't give for a debauched weekend in the city pigging out at Pizza Express followed by something really tacky from Blockbuster! But no, we had to traipse off to another community last weekend — I think it was Yorkshire or maybe Lancashire, there were hills and it rained all the time. Frank got off on the wrong foot right away because he didn't even know his star sign and there was a terrible silence at lunch on Saturday when I said I'd never done any co-counselling, and then Frank said he thought the local town could do with a bypass — well, it could! — just after a bunch of them came back from protesting against it (how was Frank to know?) and I could see them looking at each other at supper when I thought Gaia was the woman who'd done the cooking but she turned out to be Gail and then I think Frank put the seal on it when he asked if anyone had a TV so he could watch Match of the Day. Somehow, I don't think they thought we were cut out for community life — and I'm not so sure they're not right!

Love, Emily

"Eeh – what a luverly bunch of coconuts"
Reproduction of Norman Gill's famous saucy seaside postcard.
Holmfirth Postcard Museum

Faery Castles in the Air

WILL ILES AND DAVID ADLER

Trying to set up a gay men's rural community proved to be very hard work indeed ...

In 1979 we both met, separately, a shepherd called Jamie Lupin, working and living by himself on an isolated Galloway sheep farm. Both of us already wanted to move away from how we lived, with family in Chorley and in a straight community in Leeds, to a new situation with gay men. Jamie put us in touch with each other and inspired the ideal of setting up not just a gay men's community, but a rural gay men's community.

This is a partial history of the hunt for a rural community for gay men, which took place with different degrees of intensity from the meeting with Jamie to the present. We authors were involved from the very start, but not in everything that took place, and our memories are bound to be faulty too, so there are bound to be things left out and remembered wrongly.

When we met in 1979 we found ourselves kindred spirits in many ways. We had both lived in communities for a good number of years, were involved in the men's anti-sexist movement and in gay politics, and we both had a sort-of vision of how a gay men's community would be both growthful personally and politically. Because we had both lived in communities, we thought we knew how to set one up and what we wanted. We must have had real enthusiasm for meetings, and for taking risks.

Together with Mike Goldsbury, a friend of David's, we went to the national Men's Anti-Sexist Conference in Bristol in March 1980 and advertised the real benefits of a rural living situation – the experiment of men living together without women's support and outside of London gay culture. There can't have been many gay men at the Bristol meeting, but there were enough for a support group, and enough that by the end of the year we had held four weekend meetings of five or six men – in Chorley, Leeds, London and Wales – and expected to set up imminently.

The most obvious problem was lack of money – none of us had any! We went to an old smithy on Exmoor, owned by a gay artist friend of a friend, who was interested in opening out his house to a group. We weren't interested: because he was most interested in sex; because it would have been us in his house; because the wonderful ideal project could suddenly have become real, with real problems – we can't remember why. We wrote to water boards and other bodies we thought might have big unused rural places they might not be using. No replies.

Our contacts with gay housing co-ops in London changed our thinking – if we became a housing co-op we'd have a much better chance of being offered empty housing for low rent. We gave up the idea of buying. And if we were near a town or city, options for work and social life would be so much better. We would be a semi-rural community. We had days of discussion over what our co-op should be called and came up with Wilde Lavender – the final 'e' of Oscar's name got dropped later.

A Housing Association in Leeds offered us a house in Chapeltown that winter, even before Wild Lavender was registered. We went to look at this huge semi-detached, semi-derelict Victorian house together. It was boarded up after someone had had a go at burning it down. The whole street, wide, tree-lined, big gardened, was due for demolition. I guess we were a bit horrified: anyway, we unanimously turned it down, saying it was too urban.

By now we were a group of about 20, with different degrees of interest in the community. A fair number of us were into the idea, wanted to see it happen, but didn't want to be the ones to move in, at least not to start with. But in January '81 enough of us felt the biggest priority was to live together as soon as possible, so we put out feelers in Leeds again. Once we were living together we could look for somewhere more rural to move on to. At the end of February we were re-offered the Sholebroke Avenue house we'd turned down the first time, promised some repairs to the fire damage, and accepted it.

we got good at sleeping through almost anything

There was room for all of us who wanted to move right away. David and Will were joined by Robert Baker, Jed Stones, Andy Dubberly and David's cat Ambi, all of us sleeping in one bedroom as repairs went on around. Visitors, sex partners, lovers all shared this communal bedroom – we got good at sleeping through almost anything.

Once settled in Leeds, jobs and social life inevitably put our plans for a rural place on the back burner. Most of our energy went on just living together: we were pretty intimate, expected more than most of us were able to give, and not very unified. There were a lot of rows. Even so, we had a wide circle of friends and acquaintances who wanted to visit and believed we did have a vision for a gay men's living group. During 1981 we went up to seven, split up and got together again, asked people to leave, and drew up guidelines for resolving difficulties. We had weekly meetings, massage, dinner parties, lots of therapy (co-counselling, Reichian, things from **In Our Own Hands**), commitment to group support. We tried a 'sleeping rota' a couple of times, spending three evenings and nights with each of the other housemates, three nights on one's own, then a meeting to discuss how we were getting on together. Eventually we got used to living together and Wild Lav, as it came to be

to living together and Wild Lav, as it came to be known, became a focus for a lot of co-op movement and gay action.

But the house was due for the bulldozer. Though we had the option of a house with a permanent cooperative there wouldn't be room for all of us – we talked of a progressive move to London, and Will moved there in 1984, though some of us remained very settled in Leeds. And the plan for a rural community was being talked about again. But what would we do in the country, and would we like being there in any case? Some Leeds people we knew had moved to Laurieston Hall, a well-established (straight) rural community in Scotland, and at a meeting there in 1984 we decided to host a gay men's week there the following summer to look at these issues.

The first Laurieston Gay Men's Week, with 20 men, was such a success that we held another, on a healing theme with a four-day fast, a few months later. Both had lots of workshops, massage, thera-

bathing, working with the community, dances and cabaret. (Gay Men's Weeks still run, at Laurieston and elsewhere, very successfully). Laurieston Hall community was an inspiration to us – a community that worked well, and was welcoming to gay men – perhaps we could run events like the weeks we'd just tried at our gay community?

By this time, Will, James Allen and Phil Clark had found another big Victorian house, also on a short-term let, in Hackney, and this became the second Wild Lav. Tim Richardson and Gerry Millar, who had lived in/been closely involved with the Leeds house, and David all moved down from Leeds to join it at the end of 1985. We became collectively vegan and inordinately house proud. Living together became increasingly successful and smooth, though the onslaught of HIV infection and the demands of lovers and impoverished jobs in workers' co-ops were also big factors. We all reckoned we'd be out of there and set up in our faery palace in the woods within a year.

Indeed, spurred by the success of the Laurieston week, things were fairly buzzing along. There were fortnightly meetings of up to two dozen of us. We visited other communities every couple of months for weekend meetings, to set up the guidelines for our community, see how others worked and get to know each other better. Circle dance was very popular. Thank you Old Hall, Beech Hill, Parsonage Farm, Lifespan, and Crabapple. We organised more Gay Men's Weeks at Laurieston and set up the Edward Carpenter Community to run them. Aims, objectives and a constitution were produced. We approached the rich and famous to be patrons (the Queen Mother and Cliff Richard never replied!). We set up a charity, based on support for lesbians and gay men, particularly those living with HIV and AIDS, in order to be able to raise money. We produced a regular Gay Men's Rural Project Newsletter. We joined and became the London contact for GRAIN, the Gay Rural Aid and Information Network.

and became the London contact for GRAIN, the Gay
Rural Aid and Information Network.

Lulworth Cove in Dorset in the spring of 1987 was
a real turning point for us. We hired a group facil-
itator for the weekend. With the group's dynamics
the focus of our attention, sharing a crowded open-
plan cliff top house, and a rush of gay men's week

mitted we were and most particularly on whether to income share. Those with personal capital felt very much under scrutiny about their intentions from those keen to income share.

The rural project group began drifting apart after that. New clusters of four or six came together to check out a new area, or follow up a collective housing need. David moved with Tim, his lover, to live at Laurieston Hall. James set up a Christian community house in London; Phil, a sister house to Wild Lav in Tooting. Others from the group explored various big houses in the south-west and East Anglia.

The original dynamic that was focused on residents of Wild Lavender had blurred and dissipated. It may be that we had had our growthful gay experience, living closely together, striving for personal and collective empowerment, building new structures and community. The process of bringing a house to fruition requires the groupwork among gay men that motivates us towards getting involved. But participation in this process was for many of us what we had been looking for all along, and we moved on to other things.

Nonetheless, some energy remained for a rural community. Will and Bernard Kelly raised money for the charity, planning a community which would run a respite centre for people with AIDS. We came close to taking on a huge weird concrete monstrosity in East Grinstead ("AIDS Duo Hit Town", said the local paper) before realising that though it might produce a community, we didn't actually want to run the respite centre or live in East Grinstead. Then, with Martin Hodge, we went through a similar process in Wales. A gay man living in a mansion house which had largely burnt down (the roof was back on, but the upper floors were a charred void) was interested in a community joining him. He was lovely, but his direction far more spiritual than ours, and after a final attuning around a waterfall we decided that it wouldn't work for us. Will then also moved to Laurieston Hall.

The dream of a rural gay men's community has remained alive, and a house in Scotland and one in Yorkshire have come close to happening in recent years. Both didn't, perhaps, because in each case one person was putting in most energy and commitment and didn't feel that input respected enough.

In a sense, the faery palace is built, and changing every year. It's not one set place, but a loose network of gay men. The palace has grown from the Gay Men's Week sense of concern, camaraderie and camp. It lives in gay men who have found themselves feeling safe outdoors together, sharing small spaces, seeing each other in repose, in distress, in fun, over a week. For most men the faery palace is a place to go on holiday, though renewing and demanding. For some it's Home – the place we feel safe returning to, but can no longer live in. For others it's the sweet memory that yearns to become more real, to open out from black and white to technicolour. Maybe one day soon all these points of expectation will find a common focus. A building with some land, a wood, some water, a sauna, a ballroom, a big kitchen. For years we both wanted to be living there as each visitor walked in the door, chopping the wood, making the tea, grounded and safe. We do these sort of things at Laurieston now. It's not the faery palace. But in a very unique way, it is a magnificent point of light on our network.

If you've read this and think "they're cynical old bastards"; well, we *are* more cynical now. If you're looking to live in a community, we think there are two options. Join an existing community. Or make a leap of faith with a place that isn't wholly right, with people who you know you'll have problems with and put your energy into making it work. Good luck!

Will Iles and **David Adler** reckon that they've told you all there is to know about them in the above article!

How to do it

Lots of people are doing it! This issue of D&D shows a boom in the numbers of embryonic communities setting up. Here we discuss some aspects of creating your very own Utopia!

Why not join an existing community?

Perhaps you've been looking at comunities for a while and not found something that suits you; certainly there don't seem to be enough communes in this country yet to cover a wide range of tastes. There is also the question of capital: there is more choice if you have it, and many don't. Perhaps you like the approach of a certain commune, but would like to live in a different area, or to bring the possibilities of the commune to your home town.

You probably don't want to re-invent the wheel, but the thought of creating your very own Utopia can be a big thrill and a real adventure – perhaps even an ego trip!

Creating an alternative lifestyle by co-operating with a bunch of other people has more possibilties in the 90s and beyond; the totally self-sufficient country house with mandatory income-sharing has given way to a spectrum with eco-villages, co-housing, shared and private incomes, shared and private ownership and a whole range of communality, which will suit many more people.

How long will it take?

Once you have a dream that you feel committed to realise, it is understandable that you want it to happen as soon as possible.

It will probably take a year or longer to set something up, although a few great opportunities can make it happen sooner. Two to five years for a place in the country seems about average, with urban communes able to assemble the ingredients more quickly, on the whole.

If it is taking more than five years, you need to ask yourself if it really is going to happen, and if the right ingredients (people, money, aims, location, property/land) are there.

Another possibility is to set up a satellite of an existing community; if there are enough people who want to join a place that is already full, this may be an easier option than to start from scratch. However, it has rarely happened "consciously" in Britain. Existing communards may have differing perceptions of the members of the "spin-off group", fearing that they will drain energy from the "mother-ship".

What are the chances of success?

As an individual, the chances of you following all the way through to living in a commune you have helped to create, are slim. As soon as you have become involved with a group of other people who are interested in the same thing, the chances improve a lot. The commune with the best chance of success is the offshoot from an existing one. For example, Twin Oaks, a large commune in Virginia (USA) propagated the community Acorn , which, after 18 months of existence looked as if it had been established for 5 or 6 years. Twin Oaks supplied employment and asked only that the new offshoot grow to accommodate 30 people in two years.

Certainly, it is harder now than in the 70s, the heyday of communal living, to get it together. In those days, large and relatively cheap country houses were easy to find and raising capital and dropping in and out of jobs was much less fraught, making the whole adventure seem less of a risk. In those days, motivation such as political or religious ideology was more of a driving force, whereas now, people, money and organisation are the biggest factors. In fact, the biggest obstacle today is raising finance, and many would-be communes fail at this hurdle.

How do I find other people?

A major problem is finding committed, like-minded people. You may be starting off with a group of friends, or you may wish to advertise right from the start.

Many groups start with 'open' meetings (at least, open within a certain interest group) and at some point close the group. A continuously open group can be very wearing as each new member will want to have their own input recognised which can result in constantly changing aims, making it harder to get past the reality barrier.

A closed group then needing more members will run into decisions as to how to select members and how to integrate them into an established group.

The size of group which works well has been endlessly discussed. It depends a great deal on the kind of commune you envisage, because there are groups out there of all different sizes. At the beginning, there will be more paperwork than later, and there need to be enough people confident with this to share the load. As the group size increases, it will be more difficult to come to decisions, but more people to action them will help keep the impetus going, and the group will be less likely to fizzle out.

"Places needing People" (see p115); "Earth Matters"; "Resurgence"; and "Kindred Spirit" classifieds; the newsletter produced by John Clark of Lifespan (see p158 for contact details) are all possible places to advertise.

How do we Organise meetings?

Meetings are critical: not just when you set up a commune, but always!

The way in which you choose to meet will vary depending on the people involved and how they have come together as well as how you plan to be together in the future. Some of the things you may want to consider are:

- How frequently to meet
- Where to meet
- How to balance business and socialising
- Use of visioning work
- Techniques to keep the impetus going
- How much involvement should children have?
- How to finance meetings and/or early administration

Don't scrimp on the structure! Although getting to know one another is vitally important, you will need structure to interact with the world and help make your dreams come true!

You may consider visiting established communes (many are glad to help, but don't end up exploiting them!), or going away on holiday together to delve deeper into shared ideals or to discover those really irritating aspects of your prospective co-communards which you realise you just couldn't live with!

How do we share the work?

Work and power are bound up together – work lends power to those who do it in this type of situation – which cuts both ways when you are trying to set up your own commune.

Work needs to be shared as much as possible, and distribution of work can often be a long-term point of debate! If you find that you are doing it all yourself, then something is going wrong. Sharing work also means sharing information and skills.

Group processes – the dynamics of the group, community building and the way you reach decisions are all important for sharing work; the more integrated you feel as a member of the group, the more likely it is that you feel confident to take jobs on.

There are different approaches to the practicalities of how work is shared, from anarchic systems to rotas, and as a group you will find what works best for you. It may be that different jobs also require different approaches – maybe you need rotas for the jobs that nobody volunteers for, or for a job that only one person is keen on, so that the work gets done and information and skills are shared. Book-keeping is the sort of job which can remain stuck with one individual for an unhealthy length of time. Adopt-a-window to paint/crop to grow/room to clean is another approach – but again it is important to move the jobs around so that people get turns at the juicy as well as the dry jobs.

There is no denying that sharing work is a big issue, and one best tackled early. You want to be sharing work as soon as there is a group, and be thinking and discussing the ways in which you will be sharing it in the future, when you finally live with one another.

What order should we do things in?

BIG IDEAS!

The main ingredients needed for setting up a commune are: people, aims, money, structure, and property/land (which will include the aspect of location).

Invariably it is the people, with their own aims, which come first. (More of how to get people together later.) Once a group has established, individual aims need to go through a sort of courtship with the aims of the group, becoming modified until there are at least some coherent ideas about what the group wants. At this point, the group may even be clear about location!

IDEAS BECOME REAL

People can "dream" endlessly about the type of place they would like to live, but when it comes to "digging", a major reality barrier is reached. It seems that money, structure and property/land lie on the far side of this barrier, and it is here that most groups founder.

The fact is that the rest of the operation cannot be tackled in a linear way. Raising money, creating a structure and finding property/land are all interconnected and need to grow together.

SUPPORTING STRUCTURES GROW

The earlier a structure can be set up, the easier it will be to raise finance – and finance will certainly affect the choice of property. Legal structures actually cost something to set up (it may be as little as £20 for a limited company), so some money will need to be raised simply on trust to start with.

The reality barrier is also a committment barrier, and will probably reduce the size of the initial 'dreaming' group. One model which is helpful in looking at the process is that of the growing tree as visualised in the side panel; the tiny seedling is almost all vision or above-ground growth, but in order to realise the vision, roots of structure have to be developed underground to provide the earthy nutrients to feed the ideals. Thus the roots of structure and financial backing need to grow in balance with the more visible parts.

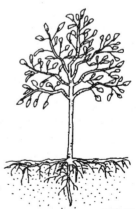

MATURE ORGANISATION
– FRUITION OF PROJECTS
– STRONG ROOTS

What about Location?

Location can be a real can of worms. There are the major decisions to take concerning urban/rural/abroad which may be difficult enough, and then there are different locations within these broad types which can often lead to loss of potential communards. Aesthetics are extremely important to some and less important to others; and what is aesthetically pleasing is so subjective (and emotional) that it may lead to rifts. Things to consider are:

- Looking for cheap housing / land above all else?
- What about schooling and losing friends?
- What are employment / business prospects?
- Are you looking for seclusion or beauty?

What Legal Structures do we Need?

Most communes find that they need about the same amount of structure as a small business. This may include a set of rules for the group as an entity (eg Memorandum & Articles for a limited company, constitution for an Industrial & Provident Society); secondary rules which are specific to the particular group; a mortgage; a business loan.

And along with this comes the necessary paperwork – minutes of meetings, book-keeping, cash-flow forecasts etc. So there seems little escape from the 'real' world! However, some groups have taken radical action in response to such legal requirements: for example, Whiteway, turning 100 years in 1998, burned their deeds a very long time ago!

What is the point of all this stuff anyway? Basically, although it seems like plugging into the system, it is a way of controlling how much the system can do to you. And it is a way of interacting with the system. For example, a bank will not be willing to lend money to a group without a copy of that group's legal structure and a cash-flow forecast which is pretty convincing. As well as being an interaction mechanism, legal structures help to clarify things: especially in the worst-case scenario when they really come into their own. And it is at this time that their use as a protector of liability also comes in handy, making it easier for groups to take risks than for individuals to do so.

For information on deciding what sort of structure will suit your group, consult Radical Routes/Catalyst Collective, your local Co-operative Development Agency or ICOM (see resources at end of this article).

How do we Share the Power?

When it comes to power, it is rare that a group getting together to set up a commune will really be on an equal footing. There are those who initiated the idea, those who have money, land or other physical resources, and those who have useful experience. Unless you have a figure who takes on the power role, and people are happy with that, it is important to either share power, or find ways to control it. The more equal the power, the easier to set up the commune.

Legal structures are a useful way in which to control power imbalances and are strongly recommended. By having a mortgage (even a private one), a loanstock agreement, or a tenancy agreement, finances can be thought of as straightforward business and do not become entangled in personal pressurising or blackmail. It is easier to separate the dream from reality when it comes to the crunch. And by having a constitution or other form of rules for running your organisation, there should be a reasonably democratic system to fall back on if needed.

A major power factor is the experience of older/founder members. These folks need to let go, which can be a very difficult thing to do, and they need to share experience so that newer people can 'catch up'.

What about Property?

The main question here is whether to self-build or renovate. Communes have quite a reputation for alternatives to standard architecture, and this tradition continues with the movement of low-impact housing and eco-villages. Walter Segal self-build designs are popular and becoming more mainstream. Communities of extremely low-cost, low-impact shelters such as benders and tipis are fighting for acceptance with planning authorities. With renovation, the group needs to decide whether to buy or rent, and decide how rents/mortgages/capital is to be met. Estate agents are an obvious place to look for property. There is even a national news sheet called 'In the Sticks' which specialises in unusual properties. (See resources at the end of this article.)

Planning permission may be an obstacle, and it is worth getting to know the planners involved at an early stage to assess what options are available. There is often room for negotiation. Planning may become easier in some places where restrictions on new-build may be due to limited resources; if you can fit into the Local Agenda 21 aspects of a council, then you may be onto a winner by turning council property into environmentally-sound housing, or by showing how water consumption can be dramatically reduced.

Council Tax is another issue to think about. Will you divide a big house into separate units, or will you live in a more communal way (multiple occupancy), which could save money?

Where can we get the money from?

How much money *do* you need? is the first question. What is your collective dream? It may be that you need to modify it in the light of financial reality!

Sources are pretty similar to those you might consider if you were starting your own business. First there are the members of the group – and there have been many large properties bought from funds raised by individuals selling their own houses. In this case, the way in which the money is pooled is important – it must be possible for people to extract money if they want to leave, but they must do it in such a way that the commune does not go into financial crisis each time someone goes. People will leave! It may seem as if you will be together forever, but when it comes to money, always have the worst-case scenario in mind and organise the paper-work accordingly.

Loan stock is a common method of pooling cash used by communities, and another possibility is to arrange a private mortgage between the commune and a member who could have security on part of the property.

If you can't borrow from within the group, think about approaching friends or relatives before you go to a bank. There is more choice these days in 'ethical' lenders, such as The Environmental Building Society, Triodos or The Co-op Bank. Such loans can be paid back by collecting rent, and business plans for such a venture should be straightforward and a relatively safe bet for such organisations to back. A really specific lender in this area is Radical Routes (see p201), an umbrella network of independent co-operatives. It raises money from sympathetic organisations and like-minded individuals, and lends to its member co-ops at very good rates.

If your organisation is a registered charity then it is worthwhile approaching trusts. There may also be ways of (positively) exploiting landfill tax legislation or renewable energy schemes.

What is Loan Stock?

Loan stock is money that is lent to the organisation (by a member or non-member) at an agreed rate of interest. Its value does not relate to the equity in the property and it is not associated with ownership of any particular part of the property. Neither does it carry with it any voting rights.

Loan stock is found within organisations that do not have shares or which have shares of a nominal value (eg £1). For example: "Companies limited by Guarantee" and "Industrial & provident Societies".

How do we pay the bills?

Communes have bills just like anyone else (although some visitors may not appreciate this!). Mortgages, council tax, maintenance, renovation, heating, light, water, sewage, food, clothing, transport and fennel toothpaste all have to be paid for somehow. There are basically two routes to go: income sharing or not. In many ways, income sharing based on trust is easier to administer, but it may bring up all sorts of anxieties about individual control; what about holidays? Is it OK to have expensive needs? Is it OK to spend more if you put more energy in? How do you define needs and wants? Is there enough trust and love for it to work? You may want to income share via an accounting system of credits – Twin Oaks (Virginia, USA) uses a complex system which has been fine-tuned over many years, but this sort of system may be too unwieldy for a small commune.

The more common route these days is for individuals to hang onto their own incomes and to pay rent and/or other contributions depending on the level of communality (see next). The ways to organise such payments is as varied as the individuals who participate.

Setting the level of rents may also be a topic of discussion – apart from covering outgoings, should they reflect market levels? How much other stuff should be included in them? Do you want low rent with the encouragement of more time spent by individuals around the commune (and if so, will this need a system to make sure jobs get done, eg paying yourselves), or are your members fully immersed in high-paying jobs and happy to pay for outside labour for things like building work? Collecting rent may be a difficult job, and one that needs to be rotated. Renters may be eligible for housing benefit – and tenancy agreements will be needed if this is the case.

How communal should we be?

This issue will come up very early, and it is extremely variable. The more communal the group is, the cheaper the living costs, and the more intense the lifestyle (at least to start with). And the closer you are as a group, the greater will be the impact when people leave or join.

Food can be a minefield when it comes to communality (will you kill your own chickens or be fruitarian? Can different eating types share the same table/frying pan/house?), and other areas (for example, childcare) which may be much more easily dealt with in a solitary or nuclear-family existence can appear to be blown out of all proportion in a communal setting. When agreements are made, it's important to get them down on paper: it's easy to forget arrangements, and when people come and go, even easier.

Access to capital if you intend to be an income-sharing group might also be tricky – can you just spend it if you have it, or should it be frozen? And what about interest; is it an income?

The balance between private and communal space varies from one place to another. Most people need some space to retreat into, but by making communal space inviting, there is the option for folk to socialise, and that might make all the difference between ending up with a commune or a shared house.

Check out these resources ➤

Must I wear a Beard?

How much people conform within a commune varies enormously. Sometimes there does seem to be a 'uniform' of sorts, although the significance of it may also vary. The safest thing to do is not to make any assumptions about a commune and likewise about prospective fellow communards – those that come together to set up a commune may not be vegetarian, non-smokers, against violence, or even hirsuit!

Think about the issues that are important to you and decide if you would find it impossible to live with someone who doesn't share your point of view. By socialising and going away together you will discover more quickly who and what you can live with, and what your own tolerance levels are!

In The Sticks
Slaggyford, Carlisle, Cumbria CA6 7NW
☎ 01434 381404
A monthly newspaper full of advertisements for wierd and wonderful properties "... by the seaside, in the forest, on the moors, in the hills ... in sleepy hamlets – far from the madding crowd – up a no through road ..." Phone for details.

The Free Land and Property Book
by John Fortune
Success Books, Maple Marketing (UK) Ltd, 11 Knowsley Avenue, Southall, Middlesex UB1 3AX
☎ 0181 813 9868
"... you can claim valuable land and property in your area and make it yours. You might not believe that this is possible. In fact it is ..." Phone for current price.

Salvo
Salvo, Ford Woodhouse, Berwick upon Tweed TD15 2QF
☎ 01668 216494
A directory of architectural antiques and reclaimed building material suppliers. £5.75 inc p&p.

What are the Pitfalls?

Each of the headings in this section highlights some kind of pitfall. The following are some of the more common ones:

- By going for immediate need you lose out on the longer-term dream.
- By not thinking things through you get into muddled financial or organisational states.
- The group never consolidates to move forward, perhaps by keeping meetings open when they should be closed.
- People get cold feet as the project becomes real.

Other pitfalls are falling out with people that you thought you knew better, and the risk of losing money that has not been secured. Such pitfalls can largely be avoided by keeping your eyes open, keeping 'real', and understanding what is happening with finances and legal structures at all times. You also need courage!

Can we get Help from Existing Communes?

Some communes are enthusiastic about helping others set up, and may provide space for meeting and share their experience, but don't assume that all will. If you want to meet at an existing commune, you may have to pay.

Some communes may be into the idea of setting up satellites, and you may find yourself in a long waiting list for a popular place where this would be a real possibility.

Again, Radical Routes is a network which facilitates the growth of the co-operative movement, and may be hepllful in terms of advice on legal matters and finance.

Legal Structures Glossary

UNINCORPORATED
If you do not "incorporate" you are viewed in law (and by the Inland Revenue) as a partnership. If things go wrong financially you are personally liable either as one of the partners (or trustees if you're also a charity).

INCORPORATED
A corporate body has a legal identity which is distinct from its members ...
Industrial and Provident Society
Each member has a £1 voting share and £1 is the limit of their liability. Money lent to the organisation by individuals is known as loan stock. The Constitution defines how the organisation functions.
Company Limited by Guarantee
There are no shares but each Director's liability is usually limited to £1. Money lent to the organisation by individuals is known as loan stock. Voting rights will be specified in the Memorandum and Articles of Association.
Company Limited by Shares
Money invested in the company is known as shareholdings. People have different shareholdings and voting rights corresponding to the number of shares which they own. The value of the shares varies according to the value of the company.

REGISTERED CHARITY
A charity does not have to be incorporated but if the Trustees decide that they want limited liability then they can incorporate as a Company Limited by Guarantee (or more rarely as an Industrial & Provident Society)

USEFUL ADDRESSES
Accountants
Janet Slade & Co
Fourways House, 57 Hilton Street, Manchester M1 2EJ © 0161 236 1493
Simon Erskine & Co
24 Plympton Street, London NW8 8AB © 0171 706 3909
Solicitors
Malcolm Lynch
Vassalli House, 20 Central Road, Leeds LS1 6DE © 0113 242 9600
James Sinclair Taylor & Martin
9 Thorpe Close, Portobello Road, London W10 5XL © 0181 969 3667
Legal Structure Experts
Radical Routes – Catalyst Collective Ltd
PO Box 5, Lostwithiel, Kernow PL22 0YT © 01726 815649
Industrial Common Ownership Movement
Vassalli House, 20 Central Road, Leeds LS1 6DE
© 0113 246 1737

POST C

Friday, Dear Jane,

Oh joy! Oh bliss! Here I am in Charing Cross Hospital with a major life-threatening illness (visiting hours are 6.30-8.30 – hint, hint!) and I can't tell you how relieved and happy I am! Why? Because Frank and I can't go visiting any more communes, or communities or co-ops or collectives or chicken coops or all those other C-words! Don't worry – I don't think I'm going to die! But it seems that Frank and I picked up a really heavy strain of Hepatitis C at that community up in Yorkshire (I'll bet it was cross-species infection from the sheep!) and now all the letters I've been writing asking to visit more communities are coming back marked "Return to Sender" and "Gone Away" or "Not Known at This Address! Anyway, three other members of our potential community group have emigrated to Greenland, two have gone to live in a caravan with Sister Wendy and the family with four kids is doing a fly-on-the-wall documentary about the Search for Community (even though they haven't found one) with Kelvin MacKenzie and the News Bunny. Frank and I have agreed to become stakeholders in something. Any ideas? **Love, Emily**

St George's Hill Golf Club, Surrey (photo: C Richard)
London's Scenic Environs

Directory of Communities and Networks

The snows melts at Old Hall Community in Suffolk

Within the UK

This first section of the Directory lists existing UK communities that have chosen to have entries. Some of these groups may work together, some may income share, some may have a spiritual focus, some may not necessarily live under the same roof; whole groups or people within the groups may be committed to ideals such as permaculture, veganism, home education and struggling against sexism, racism and homophobia; others may well not.

Please bear in mind that there are many other communal groups who are not listed, including countless urban house-shares, but all the groups in this directory share a desire to be public about their lifestyle; many are looking for new members, and most of them welcome visitors. If you are thinking of setting up a new group, or joining an existing one, this is the place to start. If you are planning to visit one of these groups for the first time then please soak up the points in the adjacent panel. Whatever you do, please don't just turn up. Remember that you will be going into people's homes, and it is important to write to them and wait for an invitation to come. You will find that some groups set aside particular times for welcoming first-time visitors. Yet again some of these communities host a whole range of workshops, courses and working weekends and you may find these a good way of visiting for the first time, although you probably won't get a flavour of day-to-day com-munal life. Don't be shy of visiting, though; most groups rely on a stream of visitors to find the new members that are essential for the ongoing life of the community.

How to use the Index, Map and Directory

The Index on pages 118 and 119 details nine features which help distinguish different types of groups. This is not meant to be a 'scientifically sound' classification, but should help

Places needing People is produced on a six-monthly basis and is mailed out with copies of Diggers and Dreamers that are purchased by mail order. It is intended to give a more immediate picture of which communities are currently looking for new members. It is not available on subscription but further copies can be obtained by sending a supply of stamped addressed envelopes. Please use "1st" or "2nd" stamps rather than those with specific monetary values.

Diggers & Dreamers, care of Edge of Time, BCM Edge, London WC1N 3XX

Visiting a Community – Points to Remember:

- visitors are important for most communities

- visitors are also where new members come from

- different communities have different approaches towards visitors

- all communities prefer you to arrange a visit and not just to turn up

- a community is home for its members; they all have their own lives, work and responsibilities to get on with so don't expect 100% of everybody's time and attention

- the atmosphere in a community will vary from day to day and is generated by all sorts of factors

- if you happen to visit on a "not terribly good day" then it is unlikely to be "your fault"

- communities have a lot of visitors and if you feel neglected it is unlikely to be because members are consciously neglecting you

- communities, generally, welcome criticism but there is a limit and it helps if, first, there is some attempt to understand not only how things are but also why

- if you want to visit again, the members will usually want to discuss this amongst themselves

- if a community doesn't want you to return it could be for any number of reasons – try not to take it too personally and keep on looking for one where you will fit in

- help with the washing-up will always be appreciated!

when selecting the groups you may wish to visit. We have gone, as far as possible, by groups' own answers to the questions. A ■ is only shown in the Income sharing?, Capital needed?, Smoking Policy? and Communal meals? columns if their answer was definitely "yes". If their answer was "no" or ambiguous then nothing is shown. In those cases it might mean, for example, that they do income share in some way or that they do eat communally occasionally. Where a group's diet is shown as vegetarian (vtn) it means that they never, ever consume any meat (although there's often some ambiguouty around fish); and where it is vegan (vgn) that they never, ever consume any animal products.

A letter denotes those communities with a spiritual focus:

A	Anthroposophy (philosophy of Steiner)
B	Buddhist
C	Christian
H	Hindu
Q	Quaker
S	Spiritual but non-specific

The numbers on both the index and the map refer to the page number of each group's entry (a couple of communities did not wish to be shown on the map). Entries are ordered alphabetically (we scrapped the regional format in D&D 96/97 as too complicated). Where a community has a link with other communities of the same generic type or its philosophy is included in its name, its geographical location is given first followed by the generic name/philosophy. This may not necessarily be the "official" name of the community (eg Aston Lee Abbey Household is a part of the Lee Abbey Fellowhip, its "official" name is Lee Abbey Aston Household Community).

Quite a lot of groups do not wish their telephone numbers to be published, in these cases we've left a gap so that you can write it in yourself when you know them on more "intimate" terms. As you will see, some communities have a very clear Ideological focus whereas others have found it impossible to answer this question and have left that part of their entry blank. The question Open to new members? is a general one. A group that is closed indef-initely will answer "no". However a group which is open in principal to new members (and therefore answers "yes") may not necessarily have any spaces at the time at which you contact them.

Disclaimer

Reading through the directory you may decide that some entries push the boundaries of communalism some-what. The editorial team has always decided that it should trust the groups and allow them to decide, themselves, whether or not they should be includ-ed. We must point out that we cannot take responsibility for the accuracy of entries, as we are not in a position to verify information sent to us, nor can we be held responsible for anything that may occur to individuals visiting groups as result of reading this direc-tory. Good luck!

	location	number of adults	number of children	income sharing?	capital required?	smoking policy	daily communal meals?	dietary regime	spiritual focus	page no
The Abbey	rural	6				■	■	vtn	C	121
Centre for Alt Tech	rural	6	2				■	vtn		122
Aston Lee Abbey	urban	6	0	■		■	■		C	123
Beech Hill Community	rural	20	5			■	■			124
Beeston Comm House	urban	6	0			■	■	vtn	C	125
Bhaktivedanta Manor	rural	52		■		■	■	vtn	H	126
Birchwood Hall	rural	9	1			■	■	vgn		127
Blackcurrent	urban	6	2			■	■	vtn		128
Bradwell Othona	rural	250	150			■	■		C	129
Brambles	urban	5	5	■		■	■	vgn		130
Braziers Adult College	rural	14	4			■	■			131
Brotherhood Church	rural						■	vtn	C	132
Burton Bradstock Othona	rural	6	0			■	■	vtn	C	133
Canon Frome Court	rural	29	19		■					134
Chicken Shack	rural	8	1							135
Christ the Sower	rural	11	5			■			C	136
Clanabogan Camphill	rural	50	12	■		■	■		A	137
Community Creation	urban	8	0				■	vtn		138
Cornerstone	urban	14	3			■	■	vtn		139
Crabapple Community	rural	5	4			■	■			140
Craigencault Farm	rural	7	0			■	■			141
Darvell Bruderhof	rural	157	146	■		■	■		C	142
Earthworm	rural	7	6				■	vgn		143
Findhorn Foundation	rural	130	20		■	■	■	vtn	S	144
Frankleigh House	rural	10	10		■	■				145
Glaneirw Commune	rural	10	5	■			■			146
Govindadwipa Dhama	rural	16	14		■	■	■	vtn	H	147
Graigian Community	urban	3	0	■		■	■	vtn	S	148
Grail Community	urban	22	0	■			■		C	149
Grimstone Community	rural	11	6	■	■	■	■	vtn	S	150
Gwerin	urban	16	1				■			151
Inverness L'Arche	urban	40	3			■	■		C	152
Juniper Communities	urban	11	0				■			153
Keveral Farm	rural	14	2				■			154

location	number of adults	number of children	income sharing?	capital required?	smoking policy	daily communal meals?	dietary regime	spiritual focus	page no
King of Love	rural	9				■		C	155
Lambeth L'Arche	urban	75	0		■		■		C	156
Laurieston Hall	rural	22	8				■			157
Lifespan Community	rural	3	3				■	vtn		158
Little Grove Community	rural	12	0	■			■			159
Losang Dragpa	rural	25	1			■	■	vtn	B	160
Lothlorien Community	rural	12	0			■	■			161
Lower Shaw Farm	urban	5	5			■	■			162
Mickleton Emissary	rural	30	6				■			163
Monimail Tower	rural	8	1				■	vtn		164
Monkton Wyld Court	rural	16	7			■	■	vtn		165
Mornington Grove	urban	12	2				■	vtn		166
The Neighbours	urban	7	4						C	167
NewBold House	rural	6				■	■		S	168
Newton Dee Camphill	urban	158	30	■		■	■		A	169
Old Hall Community	rural	40	20	■	■		■			170
Parsonage Farm	rural	9	5				■			171
Pathfinder Fellowship	urban	15	2			■	■		C	172
Pennine Camphill	rural	55	20				■		A	173
People in Common	rural	7	3				■			174
Pilsdon Community	rural	34	6				■		C	175
Plants for a Future	rural	8	1					vgn		176
Postlip Hall	rural	18	13	■						177
Quaker (Bamford)	rural	16	6				■		Q	178
Rainbow	urban	34	20							179
Redfield Community	rural	15	12				■			180
Salisbury Centre	urban	5	0			■	■	vtn	S	181
Shrub Family	rural	3	2			■	■			182
Simon Community	urban	40	0				■			183
Sisters of the Church	urban	17		■		■	■		C	184
Somefriends	urban	16	0			■	■	vtn		185
The Space House	urban	6	0			■	■	vtn		186
Talamh	rural	12	2			■	■	vtn		187
Taraloka	urban	9	0			■	■	vtn	B	188

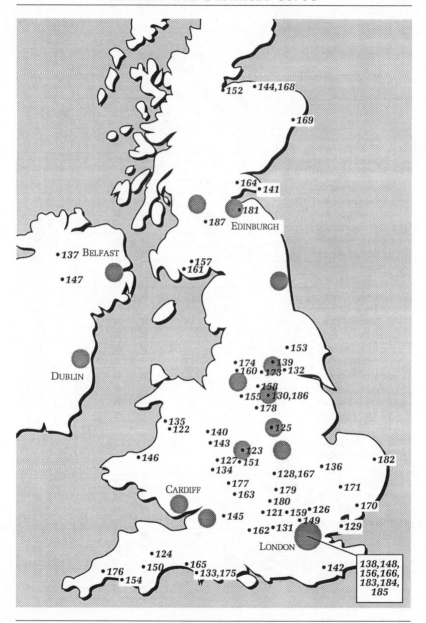

Rooted in the Christian tradition, the Abbey is a community and educational/retreat centre, offering possibilities for all who follow a spiritual path, whether or not they come from a particular religious tradition. Our everyday life is based on what is perceived as the four true relationships to: God, the earth, ourselves and others. We attempt to live in a way that is simple and ecologically sound. We share regular times for meditation and worship. We care for an interesting thirteenth century house. Rooms are available for hire. The library includes most of Gandhi's published works. The Abbey programme provides weekend and on-going courses on spirituality, inter-faith dialogue, the creative arts, alternative economics and social justice issues. There are four acres of grounds, including an organic vegetable garden. The Guest House accommodates fourteen.

THE ABBEY

Status

existing community

Address

The Green
Sutton Courtenay
ABINGDON
Oxfordshire
OX14 4AF

Telephone

01235 847401

Fax

01235 847608

Number of over 18s

6

Number of under 18s

Year started

1981

Situation

rural

Ideological focus

christian root

Legal structure

registered charity

Open to new members?

yes

CENTRE FOR ALTERNATIVE TECHNOLOGY

We're an informal group of six adults and two children (plus up to five long-term volunteers) who all work at CAT. Our main communal activity is the joint buying, cooking and eating of our food. We all have our own small houses, powered by the site's renewable energy grid; our sewage is treated by the Centre's reed beds and our water supply comes from a reservoir via our sand filter. We are therefore a demonstration of how people can live reasonably sustainably. We make decisions very late at night when we've all drunk lots of red wine. Membership is only open to those who already work at the Centre for Alternative Technology.

Status
existing community

Address
Llwyngwern Quarry
MACHYNLLETH
Powys
SY20 9AZ

Telephone

Fax
01654 702782

Electronic mail
info@catinfo.demon.co.uk

Number of over 18s
6

Number of under 18s
2

Year started
1975

Situation
rural

Ideological focus
ecological

Legal structure
unincorporated

Open to new members?
no

World Wide Web *http://www.foe.co.uk/CAT*

We are a small ecumenical Christian community of adults, part of the wider Lee Abbey Fellowship, committed to living and working in a multi-faith, multi-racial area. Our Victorian terraced house has four single and one double bedrooms, a community lounge, kitchen and bathroom all upstairs. Downstairs has facilities which can be used by others in the neighbourhood for committee meetings, quiet days etc, with a pleasant garden. We meet together for daily worship and prayer, share the tasks of cooking, cleaning, shopping and entertaining, and pool our wages or benefits, receiving a weekly amount for personal use. We share the use of the community car. We try to reach decisions by consensus, and are committed to spending time together, supporting, encouraging and listening to each other. We do paid or voluntary work, spend time with local folk, offer hospitality, and share our faith as and when appropriate. Each of us is an active member of a local Christian fellowship or church, and we want to deepen our faith. We offer a supportive, reflective, prayerful environment in which to experience life in the inner city. Enquiries by post welcome.

ASTON LEE ABBEY HOUSEHOLD COMMUNITY

Status
existing community

Address
121 Albert Road
Aston
BIRMINGHAM
B6 5ND

Telephone

Number of over 18s
6

Number of under 18s
0

Year started
1988

Situation
urban

Ideological focus
christian

Legal structure
registered charity

Open to new members?
yes

BEECH HILL COMMUNITY

Status
existing community

Address
Beech Hill House
Morchard Bishop
CREDITON
Devon
EX17 6RF

Telephone
01363 877228

Fax
01363 877228

Number of over 18s
20

Number of under 18s
5

Year started
1983

Situation
rural

Ideological focus
ecological

Legal structure
company limited by guarantee

Open to new members?
yes

B eech Hill is a spacious country house set in the rural heart of Devon. There are also a number of outbuildings converted for living in and for projects of interest to the co-op. We have seven acres of grounds and gardens. All cultivation is organically based and is largely focused upon production of a wide variety of vegetables and fruits. We have a young vineyard, a plant nursery, an ancient walled garden and a large paddock. A new course centre provides accommodation and facilities for paying guests and groups. Some of us earn a living outside and some work within the co-operative. To live here happily and effectively, people need goodwill, personal initiative, tolerance and stability. Dogmatism and preaching are definitely not wanted. Our intention is to go beyond narrow definitions of party politics, religious tradition and social structure. The co-operative's aims are summed up as follows: (1) to achieve maximum flexibility for individuals within collective policies, (2) to enable people to use and develop skills, (3) to provide a meeting place where people can share ideas, information and experience, (4) to create structures and opportunities which maximise possibilities within the current social and economic climate and (5) to be aware of the impact of our work and lives on the environment and to develop projects accordingly. We welcome visitors – please send an sae for more information.

Beeston Community House is a group of six Ecumenical Christians, five of whom contribute part of their income to support the sixth, in full-time voluntary community work. The members aim to live as a community, eating together and generally participating in work and social events as a group, sharing an interest in exploring vocation and lifestyle while recognising that people need time for themselves and their own interests. The community is Ecumenical and includes people from varying backgrounds and traditions, but all are committed as Christians to serving the local community, exploring discipleship and Christian lifestyle and to work for church unity.

BEESTON
COMMUNITY
HOUSE

Status
existing community

Address
4 Grange Avenue
Beeston
NOTTINGHAM
NG9 1GJ

Telephone

Number of over 18s
6

Number of under 18s
0

Year started
1975

Situation
urban

Ideological focus
ecumenical

Legal structure
registered charity

Open to new members?
yes

BHAKTIVEDANTA MANOR

Status
existing community

Address
Dharum Marg
Hilfield Lane
Aldenham
WATFORD
Hertfordshire
WD2 8EZ

Telephone
01923 857244

Fax
01923 852896

Electronic mail
bhaktivedanta.manor@
com.bbt.se

Number of over 18s
52

Number of under 18s

Year started
1973

Situation
rural

Ideological focus
vaishnava

Legal structure
registered charity

Open to new members?
yes

Bhaktivedanta Manor is the main centre of the International Society for Krishna Consciousness in the UK. It is 67 acres of gardens, lake, woodland and pastures. Over 100 single students of Krishna consciousness study and serve at the Manor with other families participating also in daily services and activities (140 members and their children live in the local area). The spiritual focus is the worship of Radha-Krishna in the traditional Vaishnava style. All meals are lacto-vegetarian and the grounds supply a lot of the flowers and vegetables needed for the community. A herd of lifetime-protected cows and bulls provide the milk and the muscle for hauling and ploughing on the site. The Manor is open for new members, but all devotees living on the property must be willing to comply with the basic standards of the community - no meat-eating, no intoxication of any type (including cigarettes, tea, coffee), no gambling and no pre- or extra-marital sex. The lifestyle of Krishna consciousness involves an awakening of the realisation that we are not these material bodies, we are the spirit soul within, the eternal children of God whom we know as Krishna. By chanting the holy names of Krishna and serving to our best capacity and devotion, we can uncover our true spiritual personalities and discover the pure love of God. We finally won our 15 year campaign for a new access drive which allows visitors to continue attending worship and classes.

World Wide Web *http://www.iskcon.org.uk/*

Birchwood Hall is a rural housing co-operative set in the Malvern Hills on the Herefordshire - Worcestershire border. Made up of The Coach House and The Main House, we live mostly separately and this description relates to the latter. Currently, the Main House group consists of nine adults and one child (5 in May 1997) and we are actively seeking new members. We all have at least part-time employment and are either based at home or travel to Malvern, Worcester or Birmingham. Jobs are: architect, potter/photographer, civil servant, environmental trainer, designer, development educator, sports administrator, environmental surveyor and university lecturer. Our work is important to each of us. We operate a degree of income sharing, paying a rent partially related to our individual incomes. Children live here free. New members do not buy into the community, neither do they take out any money when they leave. Our home, the Main House, is a large Victorian Hall and consists of a mix of communal and personal space. Each member can have his or her own room, while we share a living and dining area, kitchen, television room, games room, laundry, three bathrooms and workshop. Everyone takes a turn in cooking the evening meal and it is at this time that we all meet daily and catch up with each other. We can sometimes live quite separately, although shared pleasures can include building and maintenance days, shopping, woodburner stocking, volleyball, table-tennis, Scrabble, gardening, walking to the pub, trips to the cinema and cleaning. Our home is set in nine acres of land, mostly woodland but we also have flower, fruit and vegetable gardens, an orchard, courtyard, volleyball pitch and a small residential centre called Anybody's Barn. The group operates on weekly business and feelings meetings and we aim to make decisions by consensus. Harmony is valued by us all. If you would like to find out more about us, write with some details about yourself and we will send you a copy of our handout, with the possibility of a visit to follow.

BIRCHWOOD HALL COMMUNITY

Status
existing community

Address
Storridge
MALVERN
Worcestershire
WR13 5EZ

Telephone

Fax
01886 884204

Number of over 18s
9

Number of under 18s
1

Year started
1970

Situation
rural

Ideological focus
left/feminist/green

Legal structure
industrial & provident society

Open to new members?
yes

BLACKCURRENT HOUSING CO-OP

We are a housing co-op with two houses in urban Northampton with six members at present plus some part time children. We have weekly meetings where all decisions are made by consensus. We are founder members of Radical Routes – a secondary co-op. Our members are all vegetarian and we eat at least one meal a day communally. We have two halls which are used as workshops, meeting spaces for gatherings and occasional fayre type events. We also have allotment plots. We are all responsible for the maintenance of the buildings, accounts, raising of loan stock, administration etc. This involves a degree of skill sharing. An organic vegetable delivery service is run by some of us, and obviously we have our own interests as diverse as greenwood-working, music, playing board games, saving the world and bad jokes. We have visitors weekends about once a month. All enquiries welcome.

Status
existing community

Address
24 St Michael's Avenue
NORTHAMPTON
NN1 4JQ

Telephone
01604 33203

Number of over 18s
6

Number of under 18s
2

Year started
1988

Situation
urban

Legal structure
industrial & provident society

Open to new members?
yes

Small core community now being established (the vast majority of members do not actually live on site). Providing atmosphere of honest acceptance and an environment where faith and life can be studied with a view to more positive action in world affairs. Hope to promote deeper understanding of our multi-faith society. Live together in one building, own room. Possible work part/full time locally but commitment needed to the aims of community. Interpersonal decisions decided one to one, other decisions dealt with by committee structure of elected members. Rural position isolated by sea, new and old buildings. Environmentally interesting site. Own reed-beds, electricity. Wish to promote use of available land, not good quality. Fluctuating numbers over a year, peaks Christmas, Summer, can be as few as six residents. Must be able to cope with variety of ages, faiths, nationalities. No facilities for childcare on site, local school nearby. Disabled facilities, share cooking, cleaning, maintenance tasks. Willing to respond to inquiries from applicants by letter.

BRADWELL OTHONA COMMUNITY

Status
existing community

Address
East Hall Farm
East End Road
Bradwell-on-Sea
SOUTHMINSTER
Essex
CM0 7PN

Telephone
01621 776564

Electronic mail
othona@
nodeknot.demon.co.uk

Number of over 18s
250

Number of under 18s
150

Year started
1946

Situation
rural

Ideological focus
christian

Legal structure
registered charity

Open to new members?
yes

World Wide Web *http://www.nodeknot.demon.co.uk/othona.htm*

BRAMBLES HOUSING CO-OP

Status
existing community

Address
82 Andover Street
Burngreave
SHEFFIELD
S3 9EH

Telephone
0114 279 7164

Fax
0114 279 7164

Number of over 18s
5

Number of under 18s
5

Year started
1991

Situation
urban

Ideological focus
ecological

Legal structure
industrial & provident society

Open to new members?
yes

Brambles Housing Co-op was formed in 1991, initially as a men's supportive co-op. However, it has evolved into a mixed co-op with sustainable and ecological (permaculture) aims. We live in two large houses in inner city Sheffield with large gardens. Brambles Resource Centre operates from the ground floor of one of the houses. The Centre is broadly aimed at enabling people (including us!) to take more control over their lives – housing, work, education, health. We aim to be off benefits by running a worker co-op. Some of the children here are home-educated and we offer advice and information on this. We are communally vegan and aim to eat together once a day. We income share and childcare share. We are and have helped set up a local mutual aid scheme. We grow a lot of our own vegetables on four allotments shared with others in the local Peasants Collective. All decisions are made by consensus. We are open to new members and also to people interested in living in the area and joining in with the various community networks. We are a fully mutual housing co-op and no capital is required to join us.

Braziers is a resident community and a non-resident network of interested associates and members. It was founded in 1950 as a registered Friendly Society with the official title of "Braziers Park School of Integrative Social Research". The main aim is to carry out group research into positive health and holistic living, seeking new ways of working and thinking together which could offer hope of further human progress. As part of this research and, at the same time, to have a constructive social activity which helps provide an added source of income for the group, its facilities and amenities are made open to the public as a residential adult education college for weekend seminars and summer schools. Braziers is a member of the Adult Residential Colleges Association. The community regularly includes a number of British and overseas student volunteers who, during four decades, have helped establish Braziers as an international education centre with a reputation which reaches to many parts of the world. We should add that, besides a large house and some cottages the community is responsible for some 50 acres (26ha) including an organic garden and home farm. The produce helps make the community partly self-sufficient. Despite initial difficulties such as threaten any new social venture - including having to encounter and transcend schismatic trends - the community has been able, slowly, to work out new methods of democratic communication and structure, guided when ever possible by knowledge available from sociology, social psychology and the understanding of psycho-social evolution. From our experience has emerged a method of self-counselling and self governance which Braziers calls "the sensory-executive synthesis". Booklets and research papers which record and explain the method are available on sale from Braziers. The Braziers group is ready to consider new recruits and interested visitors for short or long periods, subject to previous written application. Information leaflets and application forms are vailable from the Warden's Office.

BRAZIERS ADULT COLLEGE

Status
existing community

Address
Braziers Park
Ipsden
WALLINGFORD
Oxfordshire
OX9 6AN

Telephone
01491 680481

Number of over 18s
14

Number of under 18s
4

Year started
1950

Situation
rural

Legal structure
friendly society

Open to new members?
yes

BROTHERHOOD CHURCH

We endeavour to follow the teaching of Christ's Sermon on the Mount. We are a land based community, and we aim at self sufficiency and acknowledge the supremacy of God rather than the rule of the state. We welcome visitors at all times. We conduct our own marriage ceremonies, funerals (the first burial here was in 1921). The Brotherhood Church came into being around 1898 and moved on to the land here in 1921 and has been totally organic ever since. We have a propaganda pulpit board by the roadside on which we like to keep a topical message. We are a totally pacifist group which is an affiliate of the "War Resisters International". Our members feel that the peace witness is very important and do not shrink from the consequences of disobeying the laws of the state when they are immoral. Not all members actually live at Stapleton. There are nine trustees. We have our annual Strawberry Tea Peace Gathering (approximately 200 people) and another largish Autumn gathering. We have facilities for groups to meet. We produce a Peace Calendar each year.

Status
existing community

Address
Stapleton
PONTEFRACT
Yorkshire
WF8 3DF

Telephone
01977 620381

Number of over 18s

Number of under 18s

Year started
1898

Situation
rural

Ideological focus
christian/pacifist/
ecological

Open to new members?
yes

In a beautiful position on the west Dorset coast, Othona invites you to live for a short while as part of a friendly, accepting community. We offer retreats, family holiday sessions and special activity weeks. A simple lifestyle, home cooking, sea views, informal worship in a tranquil chapel and a sense of community. Othona has an ecumenical Christian basis. We welcome people of all faiths and none, trying to avoid barriers of age, ability, race, background, or sexual orientation. There is a resident core community of six people. Visitor charges per week for full board are £112 with concessionary and children's rates. Programme available.

BURTON BRADSTOCK OTHONA COMMUNITY

Status
existing community

Address
Coast Road
Burton Bradstock
BRIDPORT
Dorset
DT6 3RN

Telephone
01308 897130

Number of over 18s
6

Number of under 18s
0

Year started
1946

Situation
rural

Ideological focus
Christian

Legal structure
Registered Charity

Open to new members?
yes

World Wide Web *http://www.solebay.com/~stevej/burton.htm*

CANON FROME COURT

Status
existing community

Address
LEDBURY
Herefordshire
HR8 2TD

Telephone
01531 670203

Fax
01531 670203

Number of over 18s
29

Number of under 18s
19

Year started
1978

Situation
rural

Ideological focus
ecological

Legal structure
industrial & provident
society and charity

Open to new members?
yes

Canon Frome Court is a Georgian mansion owned by members of the Windflower Housing Association, who have converted the house and stable block into 18 separate living units, with communal dining, sitting and meeting rooms, kitchens, guest rooms, and hall plus a swimming pool. We don't have a shared ideological focus, though there is a prevailing sympathy with green issues. The farm is the reason most of us have chosen to live here, and we enjoy farming our land co-operatively to produce a considerable proportion of our food. We have cattle, sheep, goats, chickens and bees, a walled kitchen garden, a large greenhouse, polytunnel and orchards. Communal activities include hosting events, eating together, craft activities and trips to the pub. Members meet weekly to discuss and plan the many aspects of living here, making decisions by consensus. Working together and independently on communal tasks is what "community" means to us. We try to find a balance between the private and the communal and depend on tolerance and flexibility to pursue our shared aims. It's not always easy but the successes are enormously satisfying and with every new member we become a slightly different community. It's never boring!

Chicken Shack is a housing co-op and permaculture site in mid Wales. We moved into Brynllwyn in August 1995 with the help of a Radical Routes loan, our own loan stock issue and a mortgage from Triodos. Most of us have taken a full Permaculture Design course and we aim to design for the land, the organisation of the community and our individual lifestyles. We spent our first year focusing on home, people and planting over 1000 native trees. Now after a 'year of observation' we feel ready to begin on our ever growing design for the land - four beautiful acres in Snowdonia National Park including a large boggy field, a meadow and a wooded area, giving us plenty of scope for creative and productive habitat management. This year we're hosting our second Permaculture Design course. We're a mixture of single people, couples and families who have weekly meetings, organise communal work and play, share resources and make decisions by consensus. We're part of a wider community which has grown up around the Centre for Alternative Technology and which exchanges labour and resources locally and we're presently host to the national administrative office of the Permaculture Association (Britain).

CHICKEN SHACK HOUSING CO-OPERATIVE

Status
existing community

Address
Brynllwyn
Rhoslefain
TYWYN
Gwynedd
LL36 9NH

Telephone
01654 711655

Electronic mail
pcbritain@gn.apc.org

Number of over 18s
8

Number of under 18s
1

Year started
1995

Situation
rural

Ideological focus
permaculture

Legal structure
industrial & provident society

Open to new members?
yes

COMMUNITY OF CHRIST THE SOWER

The Community of Christ the Sower is an ecumenical Christian Community of families and single people based at Little Gidding in cambridgeshire and inspired by the seventeenth century church founded by Nicholas Ferrar. The little church, visited by T S Eliot in 1936, is open daily to visitors. The parlour, serving tea and cake is open on Friday, Saturday and Sunday from 2 to 5 pm. We have four guest rooms and facilities for groups to meet.

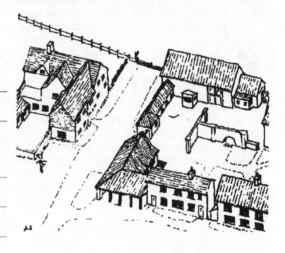

Status
existing community

Address
Little Gidding
HUNTINGDON
PE17 5RJ

Telephone
01832 293383

Fax
01832 293589

Number of over 18s
11

Number of under 18s
5

Year started
1981

Situation
rural

Ideological focus
christian

Legal structure
registered charity

Open to new members?
yes

In this therapeutic community, adults who have difficulties arising from mental and emotional disability live and work together with co-workers and their children. Agriculture and horticulture (biodynamic) are very important activities in the community and provide healthy and meaningful work as well as enhancing people's awareness of the environment. Home produce is consumed. Baking, weaving and other handicrafts are being developed in workshops. Co-workers join Clanabogan as volunteers and do not receive wages, their material needs being met from a common fund. In all aspects of life and work, mutual agreement is the basis of a committed and responsible involvement. Camphill Communities are Christian and nondenominational and many festivals are celebrated socially and artistically throughout the year. A cultural life is built up together with music, drama and lectures of an educational nature taking place regularly. Many of these activities as well as the therapeutic principles used are inspired by anthroposophy, a philosophy originating in Europe with Rudolf Steiner. This is an attempt to live a new kind of community life to include people of many nationalities and people with different problems, strengths and weaknesses. Most people find they meet interesting and rewarding experiences, learn new skills, grow and develop.

CLANABOGAN CAMPHILL COMMUNITY

Status
existing community

Address
15 Drudgeon Road
Clanabogan
OMAGH
County Tyrone
BT78 1TJ

Telephone
01662 256111

Fax
01662 256114

Number of over 18s
50

Number of under 18s
12

Year started
1984

Situation
rural

Ideological focus
anthroposophical

Legal structure
registered charity

Open to new members?
yes

COMMUNITY CREATION

Status
existing community

Address
Battlebridge
LONDON
NW1 2TL

Telephone
0171 278 7172

Fax
0171 713 5657

Number of over 18s
8

Number of under 18s
0

Year started
1992

Situation
urban

Ideological focus
ecological

Legal structure
company limited by guarantee

Open to new members?
yes

The Community Creation Trust, founded and directed by Julie Lowe, is now established as a charity dedicated to environmental education, in building design and human behaviour generally. The Trust has been given a four-year lease of a 1.5 acre site behind Kings Cross Station, London, with buildings which include a long concrete barn. Here the Battle Bridge Centre is coming to life. Timber chalets will be constructed to house 16 homeless people and to create within the barn a green village with a vegetarian restaurant, conservatory, resource centre, shops, offices, workshops and the RAJA Project, a holistic health service offering a wide range of therapies and including a detoxification programme. A large auditorium in the centre of the barn will be used for exhibitions, fairs and inter-faith events. A demonstration eco-house will be open to school children and other visitors. The development has started on site with the aid of volunteers and gifts of materials and cash. The aim is to address specific local problems, which include homelessness, drug addiction, unemployment, and partially derelict locality; and to offer some services to a wider public via the eco-house and Raja. The Trust is also helping to set up a resource centre in Tamil Nadu, India. Offers of help or participation in any shape or form are welcome.

Cornerstone owns two properties in Chapeltown, Leeds. It was formed in 1993 to house people working for social change. Our members include protesters, writers, campaigners, teachers, printers, architects and students. There is a range of spiritual beliefs from humanism to buddhism and paganism. We are renovating our houses along ecological lines, to incorporate renewable fuels, energy conservation and waste recycling. We are applying permaculture principles to our large gardens, and we are starting to get some of our food from them. We have a community resource centre which provides facilities (computers, e-mail, photocopying) and information (especially on co-ops and environmental issues) to our members and the local community. At the other house, the cellar houses gardening equipment, a craft workshop and a printing press. We are a member of Radical Routes, a national secondary co-op for co-ops working for social change. We provide a national point of contact for enquiries. Our communal kitty provides food and consumables, but we don't at present income share. All our members are vegetarian or vegan, and live low consumption lifestyles. We have monthly meetings, and feelings meetings to help us stay in touch; most members hold an officer post.

CORNERSTONE HOUSING CO-OPERATIVE

Status
existing community

Address
16 Sholebroke Avenue
Chapeltown
LEEDS
West Yorkshire
LS7 3HB

Telephone
0113 262 9365

Electronic mail
cornerstone@gn.apc.org

Number of over 18s
14

Number of under 18s
3

Year started
1993

Situation
urban

Ideological focus
environmental &
social justice

Legal structure
industrial & provident
society

Open to new members?
yes

CRABAPPLE COMMUNITY

Status
existing community

Address
*Berrington Hall
Berrington
SHREWSBURY
Shropshire
SY5 6HA*

Telephone

Number of over 18s
5

Number of under 18s
4

Year started
1976

Situation
rural

Legal structure
*industrial & provident
society*

Open to new members?
yes

Our assets include a Georgian rectory (1805) in good repair with 14 bedrooms, two kitchens, two large communal rooms and one for hire, three harmoniums, weaving looms, spinning wheel, dairy equipment, solar panels, ping-pong table and seven cats. Outside we have under-used outbuildings, two yards, a workshop, garage, pottery, farm machinery, Dutchbarn and usually some old cars, in 20 acres with a walled garden, children's play areas, polytunnels, greenhouses, established woodland, young coppicing, new willow bed, lilacs in April, sixty hens, 15 sheep, beehives, wisteria, fruit trees, a compost toilet and a camp site. Human assets aged from 4 to 49 are three young children, one teenager, five adult members, sundry WWOOFers, visitors and friends. We're committed to common ownership, organic gardening and farming, concensus decision-making and a co-operative lifestyle. We pay basic rent and board but with most people would aim for a more proportional income sharing. Crabapple Wholefoods is now run by a worker co-op and not by us so we are looking for new members who will be able to generate their own income, possibly from here, and have time, energy and enthusiasm for sharing the maintenance and development of the community. Please write for details telling us a bit about yourself.

Craigencalt is a smallholding of 23 acres beside Kinghorn Loch with views south over the Forth estuary and is made up of organic market garden, orchards, poultry range, permanent pasture and woodland which we have planted. The extensive steading has wood and metalwork workshops, a meeting/ceilidh barn and an art studio and more space to use. Additional outbuildings exist as well. The large house is home to seven members living communally and the community also has two members living locally. The age range is mid twenties to late seventies. The house is run on equal contributions to costs and shared work. The property is currently owned by two of the members but we are working towards creating an ecological centre which would assume ownership when possible. Decisions are taken communally at a weekly meeting. Local community involvement has been achieved through formation of an advisory group. We have a steady flow of working visitors of all ages and nationalities whose assistance is always very welcome. Meditation is important to our life and we share a Quaker style meeting on Sundays which also provides space to deal with personal issues not appropriate to the business meeting.

CRAIGENCAULT FARM

Status
existing community

Address
Craigencault Farm
KINGHORN
Fife
KY3 9YG

Telephone

Fax
01592 890078

Electronic mail
Richard_Neil@
compuserve.com

Number of over 18s
7

Number of under 18s
0

Year started
1989

Situation
rural

Ideological focus
ecological

Open to new members?
yes

World Wide Web *http://ourworld.compuserve.com/homepages/Richard_Neil/craigf.htm*

DARVELL BRUDERHOF COMMUNITY

Status
existing community

Address
*ROBERTSBRIDGE
East Sussex
TN32 5DR*

Telephone
01580 883300

Fax
01580 881171

Electronic mail
ploughuk@bruderhof.com

Number of over 18s
157

Number of under 18s
146

Year started
1920

Situation
rural

Ideological focus
christian

Legal structure
registered charity

Open to new members?
yes

The Bruderhof Community began in Germany in 1920 just after the First World War, when Eberhard and Emmy Arnold with their five children moved to the village of Sannerz from their comfortable home in Berlin, to start a life of radical discipleship. Our roots go back 460 years to the Anabaptist movement, indeed to the Early Christians of the first 200 years AD and we seek to live like them. There are Bruderhof Communities in England and in the United States. Membership requires a lifetime commitment. Our first call is to Christ and this cannot be separated from the brothers and sisters to whom we are pledged. We do not feel that any one pattern for daily life is the answer, but we do believe in a life of Christian brotherhood that is the fruit of an inner change of heart. Our desire is to follow Jesus in the spirit of purity and humility in every aspect of life. Bruderhof children are educated in our own schools up to high school age. Training beyond that age is received outside the community, in most instances. The principal means of livelihood is our manufacturing - Community Playthings, nursery school equipment and "Rifton Equipment for the Disabled". In addition, our non-profit Plough Publishing House offers a diverse selection of books, cassettes and videos covering all aspects of Christian discipleship and life in Christian community. Write for our free quarterly, *The Plough*. Inquiries are welcomed. Visits can be arranged but please write or call in advance so as to ensure accommodation. Guests are asked to share in the work and life in an open and seeking way. Our urgent longing and hope is that all men and women on this earth will one day live in true justice and brotherhood under the rulership of God.

World Wide Web *http://www.bruderhof.org/*

A now 'experienced' housing co-op, we live and work communally at Weatstone where there's a large old house, outbuildings and seven acres; on the edge of a quite pretty Marches/Borders village. We make decisions through regular meetings and on a day-to-day basis almost always by consensus (voting only as a last resort). The group's membership and direction has undergone several changes since we arrived in 1990, but the same original principles and ideals remain, including an ecological focus, trying to be more kind to the earth, limiting use of products which pollute and poison, and trying to be more ethical consumers. We 'farm' by vegan -

EARTHWORM HOUSING CO-OP

organic methods, using permaculture and forest garden techniques. We use composting loos. We grow seasonal vegetables, herbs and soft fruit in the gardens and in two polytunnels. We don't keep food animals. All communal areas and meals are vegan. You don't have to be vegan or vegetarian to live here, but it helps. We still spend much effort and money repairing the house which was badly vandalised and neglected previously. We host gatherings, courses and camps. Some of us work outside the community. We have set times for visitors/potential members; please enclose an SAE when writing.

Status
existing community

Address
Wheatstone
Leintwardine
CRAVEN ARMS
Shropshire
SH7 0LH

Telephone
01547 540461

Number of over 18s
7

Number of under 18s
6

Year started
1990

Situation
rural

Ideological focus
ecological

Legal structure
industrial & provident society

Open to new members?
yes

FINDHORN FOUNDATION

The Findhorn Foundation is at the heart of an international spiritual community. It was founded in 1962 by Peter Caddy, Eileen Caddy and Dorothy Maclean in the belief that humanity is engaged in an evolutionary expansion of consciousness, creating new patterns of civilisation infused with spiritual values. Over the years the Foundation has grown into a major centre of adult education with more than 4000 residential visitors a year. It is also the centre of a new and developing eco-village.

Co-operation and co-creation with nature is a major aspect of the Community's work and there is no formal doctrine or religious creed. The Community has diversified into more than 30 different businesses and initiatives and provides a valuable insight into sustainable living. You are welcome to visit, live and work with the Community in a variety of ways as we explore work, relationships and the environment in new and fulfilling ways.

Come and help create a positive vision and future for humanity and the planet. Information about visits, workshops, quest programmes and conferences is available from the reception office, please write for details.

Status
existing community

Address
The Park
Findhorn
FORRES
Morayshire
IV36 0TZ

Telephone
01309 690311

Fax
01309 691301

Electronic mail
reception@findhorn.org

Number of over 18s
130

Number of under 18s
20

Year started
1962

Situation
urban & rural

Ideological focus
practice/demonstration

Legal structure
registered charity

Open to new members?
yes

World Wide Web *http://www.gaia.org/findhorn*

Frankleigh House is a co-housing community of five families, currently seeking new members. We live in a large, run-down Victorian country house with 14 acres of land, including swimming-pool and tennis court. The house is divided into separate units, mostly self-contained, and we share the communal space and the land - each family has its own allotment and we are about to start a communal garden. We have no common ideological focus but we try to be reasonably "green". At present, our common aims are to renovate the house and to live together harmoniously and sociably within the community while also leading independent family lives. Some of us do paid work from home, some outside the home and several of the children are home-educated. We have done a lot of work and the house is now comfortably habitable but there is still building work to do and we would like to start cultivating the land. All work is done voluntarily, the spirit being that there should be no pressure, no resentment. We have a monthly directors' meeting, and weekly works and "issues" meetings. We aim to make decisions by consensus but can do so with an eighty percent majority. We don't have any compulsory communal activities but we like to have fun together and meet up spontaneously for shared meals, festivities, outings etc. Please write for more information.

FRANKLEIGH HOUSE CO-HOUSING COMMUNITY

Status
existing community

Address
Frankleigh House
Bath Road
BRADFORD-ON-AVON
Wiltshire
BA15 2PF

Telephone
01225 866467

Electronic mail
100441.557@
compuserve.com

Number of over 18s
10

Number of under 18s
10

Year started
1995

Situation
semi-rural

Ideological focus
none

Legal structure
company limited by shares

Open to new members?
yes

World Wide Web *http://ourworld.compuserve.com/homepages/dmichael/*

GLANEIRW COMMUNE

Status
existing community

Address
Blaenporth
Abertiefi
CEREDIGION
SA43 2HP

Telephone
01239 810548

Number of over 18s
10

Number of under 18s
5

Year started
1975

Situation
rural

Ideological focus
ecological/
eco-emotional™

Legal structure
industrial & provident
society

Open to new members?
yes

Glaneirw is a small farm in west Wales with 44 acres of land and a large shabby house in which we live. We try to get most of our food and fuel from the land. There is a walled garden, an orchard and two polytunnels for vegetable and fruit growing. We keep cows, donkeys, chickens, ducks and geese. We have 5 acres of mature woodland and 8 acres planted since the commune began. There is a mortgage to pay so we have a business repairing, converting and supplying parts for Rayburn cookers, and a pottery workshop with our own shop. We pool our income and take weekly pocket money. Everyone has their own room but other rooms are communal. We share a meal every evening and have informal meetings every week. Housework, cooking and emptying the compost toilets, are also shared. New ventures for the year are bee-keeping and digging a drainage trench and reed bed, repairs to the buildings are ongoing. We enjoy having visitors but please write and make arrangements first. We are particularly interested in diggers and weeders, builders and alternative energy experts, but anyone with energy and humour will be welcome.

Govindadwipa Dhama is a community of the devotees of Krishna, the Supreme Personality of Godhead. Community members have a fundamental purpose for being here: to aspire to know and to love God by way of the ancient Vedic scriptures, studied under the guidance of great devotee saints. The monastery/temple is situated on a beautiful wooded island; the householders with children live nearby. The temple president, like an abbot, is in charge - but just off the island, householders live independantly. The temple is funded by donations from householders, guests and the sale of literature, such as 'Bhagavad Gita'. Community members follow strict principles; no meat-eating, gambling, intoxication and sex for procreation only. Additionally, devotees chant God's names on prayer beads; a minimum of '16 rounds' or 27,600 names of God daily. The purpose of chanting His names is to purify ourselves of bad qualities such as lust, anger, envy etc, and to gradually reawaken our dormant consciousness of God. We regularly come together to sing and chant about Krishna. Temple services begin at 4:30 am and there is a philosophy class at 7.30 am every morning. Guests are welcome to stay overnight, although accommodation is basic. Correspondence to the secretary.

GOVINDADWIPA DHĀMA

Status
existing community

Address
Derrylin
The Lake Isle of Inis
Rath
Lisnaskea
ENNISKILLEN
County Fermanagh
BT92 9GN

Telephone
013657 21512

Electronic mail
105400.2653@
compuserve.com

Number of over 18s
16

Number of under 18s
14

Year started
1985

Situation
rural

Ideological focus
Krishna

Legal structure
registered charity

Open to new members?
yes

GRAIGIAN COMMUNITY

We founded this monastic community in May 1983 out of a deep desire to have a positive effect on the world. As writers, artists, craftsmen and environmentalists we care greatly about everything we see, hear, smell and touch. All decisions have to be made democratically and unanimously! Although we live in the centre of London ... our focus, our passion, is for the countryside and everything old-fashioned and rural. We have just commenced publishing books: our first one is a hardback (price £14.60) called **The Future will be Green**. It is, in all sincerity, a manifesto, a guide book for everything we have discovered and believe in. As artists we feel strongly about everything visual! If sincere people wish to come to visit us and be shown around - then please telephone us (between 2pm and 8pm) for an appointment. We survive by selling our books, booklets, pots, candles and paintings. We have a very strict, but also delicious, vegetarian diet. We would love to meet members of other communities (whether secular or spiritual). Being practical and down-to-earth is considered vital here. Through the Twelve Archetypes of Natural Psychology (our own subject) we help vistors to this monastic house understand themselves. Co-operation and consultation are our golden rules!!!

Status
existing community

Address
10 Lady Somerset Road
Kentish Town
LONDON
NW5 1UP

Telephone
0171 485 1646
(between 2pm and 8pm)

Number of over 18s
3

Number of under 18s
0

Year started
1983

Situation
urban

Ideological focus
psychological

Open to new members?
yes

The Grail community is one of several branches of the Grail Society which started in Holland in 1921. It is a Roman Catholic institute of single and married people. The society seeks, in an increasingly impersonal world to promote understanding of the uniqueness and value of each person. The long term community at Waxwell consists of single women who make a life commitment sharing resources and observing accountability to the group.

THE GRAIL COMMUNITY

Waxwell is a listed Elizabethan house with conference extensions, set in ten acres of wooded garden. The work consists of supporting families and married people, publishing, hospitality, and workshops on arts, spirituality, stress management and the provision of space and solitude.

Short-term members and volunteers are welcome. The former share our life for a year and participate in the work of the community whilst exploring new directions. Volunteers, many from overseas, live alongside the community helping with the running of the house and upkeep of the grounds. On a daily basis, people come for activities such as weaving, spinning, study and prayer groups, healing, relaxation and yoga. Believers of all traditions and of none are welcome.

New developments in our leadership structures have prompted us to draw more readily on the generous help and expertise of our members, contacts and friends throughout the country, many of whom are frequent visitors.

Status
existing community

Address
The Grail Centre
125 Waxwell Lane
PINNER
Middlesex
HA5 3ER

Telephone
0181 866 2195/0505

Fax
0181 866 1408

Electronic mail
waxwell@
compuserve.com

Number of over 18s
22

Number of under 18s
0

Year started
1932

Situation
edge of London

Ideological focus
Christian

Legal structure
registered charity

Open to new members?
yes

Write to Wendy Daniels - who we are do what we do etc.

GRIMSTONE COMMUNITY

Grimstone Community was originally formed in 1990 to buy and develop the existing successful workshop centre at Grimstone Manor. A magical spot on the edge of Dartmoor, it is set in 27 acres of garden, pasture and wilderness. Members make a financial investment in the property and join the business partnership. We are eleven adults and six children, and one family who have joined as affiliate members, investing money as non-residential co-owners of the property. Our main focus as a community is to service the many varied self development groups who come to work in, receive and feed the special energies here.

We meet once a week, alternating business and process meetings. All decisions are taken by consensus between equal partners. Members focalise different areas of work but, generally, all work is shared and paid at the same hourly rate. Short-term volunteers work in return for their keep. We are moving towards building a sense of community on material, emotional and spiritual levels. Together, we eat daily, meditate weekly, laugh, work and grow. There are local community links through circle dancing, chanting and other events. We are open to new members with capital, flexibility and enthusiasm.

Status
existing community

Address
Grimstone Manor
Horrabridge
YELVERTON
Devon
PL20 7QY

Telephone
01822 854358

Fax
01822 854358

Electronic mail
101653.2176@
compuserve.com

Number of over 18s
11

Number of under 18s
6

Year started
1990

Situation
rural

Ideological focus
new age

Legal structure
unincorporated

Open to new members?
yes

World Wide Web *http://www.onestepbeyond.co.uk/centres/grimstone*

Gwerin is a housing community, of five houses and a total of sixteen adults and one child. Four of the houses are part of a Victorian terrace and they are fairly large. These large houses are shared by members of our community. Each house is run differently according to the individuals who make up the household. We have weekly meetings where we all come together to discuss the running of the housing association. We are a mixture of individuals and as a community have no particular ideological focus, although a large number of us have contacts with the local Rudolf Steiner school.

**GWERIN
HOUSING
ASSOCIATION**

Status
existing community

Address
*121 Hagley Road
STOURBRIDGE
West Midlands
DY8 1RD*

Telephone
01384 396582

Fax
01384 863982

Number of over 18s
16

Number of under 18s
1

Year started
1982

Situation
urban

Ideological focus
consensual

Legal structure
industrial & provident society

Open to new members?
yes

INVERNESS L'ARCHE COMMUNITY

Status
existing community

Address
care of
Diggers & Dreamers

Telephone
01463 239615

Fax
01463 711089

Number of over 18s
40

Number of under 18s
3

Year started
1975

Situation
urban

Ideological focus
ecumenical christian

Legal structure
registered charity

Open to new members?
yes

L'Arche was founded in 1964 by Jean Vanier, and welcomes people with learning disabilities and assistants. There are two communities in Scotland, integrated into local neighbourhoods in Edinburgh and Inverness. These communities are two of an international family of communities spread throughout the world.

L'Arche in Inverness started in 1975 with the opening of its first house, "Braerannoch", offering people with learning disabilities and assistants the opportunity of a permanent home and the chance to share their lives in a family-like atmosphere. Since then, the community has grown to include two other houses in Inverness, and a workshop providing choices of woodwork, craft, therapy and gardening for people with learning disabilities. L'Arche Inverness is an ecumenical Christian community welcoming people of all faiths or none. It is inspired by the Sermon on the Mount, which reveals that those who appear to have little to offer, do in fact have much to give and to share. We believe that the life of each person, regardless of their ability, is a gift. We believe each person has a unique and mysterious value, and that we all need a place to discover our own value and the value of others, to grow and to develop. This is why L'Arche Inverness aims to offer people whom society labels as 'mentally handicapped' or as having 'learning disabilities', the opportunity of a rewarding and fulfilling life in the context of a community lifestyle. The assistants who share this way of life come with the belief that through their relationships with people with learning disabilities, they will learn a great deal. You can help L'Arche in a number of ways: • by visiting the community and getting to know us. • by donating money to help provide for the material resources we need. • by considering spending time in one of the houses as an assistant. • by visiting "L'Arche Crafts & Horticulture", our workshops to buy products made there. • by joining "Friends of l'Arche Inverness" We look forward to hearing from you!

Juniper communities has had two houses in York where we provide 24 hour supported communal living for adults who have learning disabilities. We offer a challenging, supportive and caring environment where people are encouraged to work towards and acheive their full potential. We can be a permanent home or part of a gradual move to independent living. Each person is required, as far as s/he is able, to participate in the tasks to maintain their household. People access community resources with the support of our development worker, support staff and volunteers to achieve their goals via churches, colleges, universities, community centres, libraries, theatres and agricultural and horticultural establishments (not daycentres). Currently, people are studying, working or enjoying the following: literacy, numeracy, money management, farming, organic horticulture, swimming, computers, art, music, drama, ceramics, horse-riding, football, keep-fit, bingo and voluntary work. People enjoy the pub, meeting friends, bowling, cinema and regular holidays. We also have our own weaving centre. Juniper is a registered charity, a company limited by guarantee and is registered under the 1984 Registered Homes Act. We are a member of the association for residential care and support the ARC code of good practice which promotes high quality care.

JUNIPER COMMUNITIES

Status
existing community

Address
24 St Mary's
YORK
YO3 7DD

Telephone

Number of over 18s
11

Number of under 18s
0

Year started
1978

Situation
urban

Legal structure
company limited by guarantee

Open to new members?
yes

KEVERAL FARM COMMUNITY

Keveral Farm is an organic farming community situated five miles from Looe, overlooking the sea. The farm is twenty-eight acres which consists of a main farmhouse, a working forge, other outbuildings, caravans, benders, tipis, a camping area, woodland, willow coppice, walled garden, polytunnels, pasture and vegetable growing plots. This year we have launched a vegetable box scheme to supply the local community with vegetables and to provide income. We also produce firewood, charcoal, and have three goats which provide us with milk, and seven hens for eggs. We attempt to manage the farm along permaculture principles, and various different systems such as forest gardens and mulched beds are springing up around the place. We also run permaculture courses. During the summer we host childrens camps as well as running focused visitor weeks. Although we are open to visitors all year round, these enable us to put much more energy into our visitors by providing guided walks, work sessions, discussions and bonfires etc. Keveral provides a sanctuary from capitalism, land to support ourselves and an extended family environment. While sometimes this may send us running off for solitude, it also gives support and closer interaction which makes fertile conditions for personal growth.

Status
existing community

Address
St Martins by Looe
LOOE
Cornwall
PL13 1PA

Telephone
01503 250215

Number of over 18s
14

Number of under 18s
2

Year started
1973

Situation
rural

Ideological focus
ecological

Legal structure
company limited by guarantee

Open to new members?
yes

Whaley Hall is a conference and retreat centre situated at the gateway to the Peak Park. The Victorian house, set in its own grounds, has been the foundation of the Community of the King of Love, an ecumenical community of women and men, since 1979.

We welcome many different groups including religious, parish and circuit groups, caring, charitable and arts organisations, educational and professional establishments as well as individuals. We seek to provide a warm, peaceful and non-institutional atmosphere in which people may be supported in their work and refreshed and strengthened for their daily lives. Guests may follow their own programmes, those organised by the house or by mutual co-operation. Members of the Community are willing to provide confidential counsel if it is requested.

If you wish to receive details of forthcoming events please ask and your name will be added to our mailing list.

COMMUNITY OF THE KING OF LOVE

Status
existing community

Address
Whaley Hall
Whaley Bridge
HIGH PEAK
SK23 7BL

Telephone
01663 732495

Fax
01663 732495

Number of over 18s
9

Number of under 18s

Year started
1970

Situation
urban and rural

Ideological focus
christian

Legal structure
registered charity

Open to new members?
yes

LAMBETH L'ARCHE COMMUNITY

Status
existing community

Address
15 Norwood High St
LONDON
SE27 9JU

Telephone
0181 670 6714

Number of over 18s
75

Number of under 18s
0

Year started
1977

Situation
urban

Ideological focus
christian

Legal structure
company limited by guarantee

Open to new members?
yes

L 'Arche Lambeth is an ecumenical Christian community where adults with learning disabilities and their assistants live and work together. There are five community households in the West Norwood area of South London, where between seven and fourteen people share daily life. Craft workshops - weaving, gardening, stonework and candle-making - provide work for community members who have learning disabilities. Assistants support people either in their home (one of the community households) or at work. Assistants come from all over the world, whenever possible for a minimum of one year; some have made the community their long-term home. L'Arche seeks to reveal the particular gifts of people with learning disabilities who belong at the very heart of their communities and who call others to share their lives. In a divided world, L'Arche wants to be a sign of hope. Its communities, founded on covenant relationships between people of differing intellectual capacity, social origin, religion and culture, seek to be a sign of unity, faithfulness and reconciliation (from the Charter of L'Arche). For further information on becoming an assistant, please contact the Assistants' Co-ordinator.

We occupy a huge house and several other dwellings in its grounds. There are acres of woodland to manage as well as a large fruit and vegetable garden and grazing for cows, hens, bees and pigs.

About a third of the adults live singly, everyone else in 'family' groups, some conventional, some not. Most of us have part-time paid work and in many ways each adult or family is domestically and economically autonomous, but we're committed to sharing out all the (unpaid) work here, and responsibility for it, as equitably as possible. We play together too: music, pantomimes, fire festivals. In the summer, as 'Woodhall Events', we run an alternative holiday centre - please write to request a newsletter.

Each year we have three maintenance weeks, in April, June and September, when we function as a communal group and when visitors are invited to stay and join in with building maintenance, gardening, land work and domestic work. Except for personal guests, we're not able to invite people at other times, and we're not actively seeking new members, so it will usually be left to people who are interested in joining to discuss the possibility with friends they make among residents.

LAURIESTON HALL

Status
existing community

Address
Laurieston
CASTLE DOUGLAS
Dumfries & Galloway
DG7 2NB

Telephone

Number of over 18s
22

Number of under 18s
8

Year started
1972

Situation
rural

Ideological focus
none

Legal structure
company limited by guarantee

Open to new members?
yes

LIFESPAN COMMUNITY

Status
existing community

Address
Townhead
Dunford Bridge
SHEFFIELD
S36 4JG

Telephone

Number of over 18s
3

Number of under 18s
3

Year started
1974

Situation
moorland

Ideological focus
practical ecological
self-sustainability

Legal structure
industrial & provident
society

Open to new members?
yes

Lifespan Community is set in the wild and bleak but beautiful Yorkshire Moors, just off the Peak District National Park. It forms a large part of the hamlet of Townhead. We have two rows of terraced houses, nineteen in all, built at the turn of the century to house railway workers from the old marshalling yard in nearby Dunford Bridge. The houses had been uninhabited for forty years and were virtually derelict (warning: a few of the houses are still in a poor state of repair) when they were bought outright in 1974 by a group of former teachers who established Lifespan as an Educational Trust. Since 1978 we've been a housing co-op – which means that ownership is always retained by the Co-op which, in turn, is controlled by the serving members. The group has long since steered away from the Educational Trust's objectives and, for most of our history, we have sustained ourselves financially by running a printing business as a worker co-op. Unfortunately, the business had to be sold in 1993 when membership dwindled and we've since struggled to establish a core group of members committed to co-operative principles and, as yet, we have failed to replace the business ... in fact, Lifespan almost folded at the end of 1996. Following protracted legal battles to preserve Lifespan against a continued influx of ill-intentioned tenants, the remaining two members reassessed Lifespan's (and our own raison d'être and we have rewritten our constitution to ensure that, as far as possible, Lifespan will attract and nurture only genuinely community-spirited people who are also committed to the work ethic; who are peaceful, sociable, supportive and of stable dispositions; and who are prepared to do their utmost to conduct themselves in an ecologically responsible manner. We welcome working visitors throughout the year but only if our members are happy with the detailed letter of introduction that is required of all potential visitors (please send an A5 sized sae if applying to visit Lifespan – applications to visit cannot be dealt with over the phone). We'll send all applicants an introductory booklet and we'll be delighted to answer any queries that remain unanswered.

Little Grove was established in 1983 and typically has about twelve members. At present, they are all adults, aged from 27 to 70 years and about 50%:50% men and women. We are broadly "alternative" in outlook and values, but have no common ideology beyond that. We are all pretty actively involved in the world, with a wide variety of jobs. About half of us work partly or wholly from home: there is plenty of space for offices, studios and workshops, plus a thriving education centre. Some of us use the latter to run a programme of personal development courses and it is also used extensively by visiting groups. There are five acres of gardens and fields. Each member has a room or two of their own and we share bathrooms (several), kitchens, lounge, hall, television room, laundry and more. Most main meals are eaten together. House business meetings are held fortnightly and there is a monthly meeting to deal with other matters. Little Grove is in a very quiet rural setting, but close to several towns and about an hour from London. Please send a 38p stamp for full details.

LITTLE GROVE COMMUNITY

Status
existing community

Address
Grove Lane
CHESHAM
Buckinghamshire
HP5 3QL

Telephone
01494 778080

Fax
01494 776066

Number of over 18s
12

Number of under 18s
0

Year started
1983

Situation
rural

Ideological focus
various

Legal structure
industrial & provident society

Open to new members?
yes

LOSANG DRAGPA BUDDHIST CENTRE

Status
existing community

Address
Dobroyd Castle
Pexwood Road
TODMORDEN
West Yorkshire
OL14 7JJ

Telephone
01202 812247

Fax
01706 818901

Electronic mail
LosangD@aol.com

Number of over 18s
25

Number of under 18s
1

Year started
1985

Situation
rural

Ideological focus
buddhist

Legal structure
registered charity

Open to new members?
yes

Losang Dragpa Centre is a Buddhist College and Retreat Centre based at Dobroyd Castle in Todmorden. The purpose of the centre is to provide a facility where people can learn about the Buddhist way of life. The community has 25 members and is always open to more. We welcome anyone who visits to stay, either just for a relaxing break, or to attend one of our courses. Prices start from £12-50 a night for dormitory accommodation with 3 meals. We also welcome anyone who wishes to stay for a week or more on a working holiday basis: 35 hours work in return for food, accommodation and teachings. The activities of the community reflect the general philosophy of Buddhism. We lead a peaceful, happy and meaningful way of life with a focus on spiritual growth, meditation and community work. Our work projects often involve conservation work on our 24 acres of grounds. Potential residents must be sympathetic to the Buddhist way of life. The castle is based in the beautiful Calder Valley, but with easy access to Leeds, Bradford and Manchester. We welcome any telephone or written enquiries from anyone requesting more information. Office hours are from 2 to 5 pm.

Lothlorien was established in 1978. It consists of a large log house with 14 bedrooms and communal living areas. It is set in 17 acres of grounds which include organic vegetable gardens, woodland, workshops and outbuildings. In 1989, Rokpa Trust, which has grown out of Samye Ling Tibetan Buddhist Centre took over the running of Lothlorien. Its aim is to maintain a supportive community in Lothlorien, where those who suffer from mental health problems can grow and develop through participation in community life. The guiding principles of the community are hospitality, care and respect for the person, and a belief that the potential of the individual can be encouraged through a communal life in which all have a contribution to make. There are places for four live-in volunteers who play a key role in helping to create a warm, accepting atmosphere in the community. Lothlorien now employs a manager, support worker and garden co-ordinator who provide a continuity of support to the community. We have vacancies on a regular basis as we see Lothlorien as a place where people can grow and develop for a period of time (usually up to one year). People are then encouraged to move on rather than seeing Lothlorien as their long-term home. Please contact the manager by phone or letter if you have any queries.

LOTHLORIEN COMMUNITY

Status
existing community

Address
Corsock
CASTLE DOUGLAS
Dumfries & Galloway
DG7 3DR

Telephone
01644 440602

Number of over 18s
12

Number of under 18s
0

Year started
1978

Situation
rural

Ideological focus
various

Legal structure
registered charity

Open to new members?
yes

LOWER SHAW FARM

Formerly a North Wiltshire dairy farm, Lower Shaw is now a thriving and extended community whose numbers fluctuate with seasons and the years. Since 1976 it has been running educational and recreational weekend and week-long courses and events as well as hiring out its facilities to groups and organisations. It has space for up to 40 people at a time but the number of its permanent resident community is usually in single figures. Both short and long-term residents recognise that Lower Shaw's strength lies in the communal atmosphere it creates, a contribution to which is its natural and informal environment, its ramshackle but loved and cared for three acres with trees, ponds, animals, gardens and outbuildings. Its residents have many local links as well as strong national and international connections. Regular meetings are held to ensure good order, continuity and a sense of humour. It's reckoned that life is for learning at Lower Shaw Farm. (We don't yet know it all!) If you want to know more, about its work, life, courses, and events, please write with a stamped addressed envelope.

Status
existing community

Address
Old Shaw Lane
Shaw
SWINDON
Wiltshire
SN5 9PJ

Telephone
01793 771080

Number of over 18s
5

Number of under 18s
5

Year started
1976

Situation
suburban (but with three acres)

Ideological focus
humanist

Legal structure
unincorporated

Open to new members?
yes

This is a long-standing community. Yet anyone looking primarily for a good community to live in is liable to be disappointed and should probably look elsewhere. Our main reason for being together is spiritual. What we do is very much of secondary importance to how we do it. We are part of a world-wide network known as 'The Emissaries", with sister-communities in many countries. Three times a week we meet for an hour or more to consider in depth our current experience of life. We also make regular use of a technique for spiritual "attunement". The focal point of our week is the meeting held at 11am every Sunday, which is always open to the public. Living in a community is not essential to our approach to life, but it is useful because it intensifies the pressure for change. Although there is a high level of love and fulfilment among us, this is also frequently a very uncomfortable place to be: the recipe only works if we are committed to maintaining, as far as we are able, a consistent sense of vision, purpose and stable atmosphere. Emissaries share a strong respect for individual integrity and perception. In finances, each person is responsible for their own income and basic expenses, and for deciding what they donate to the community. Communal decisions are made in many and varied ways. The management of our affairs emerges from a core of agreement. We all accept responsibility for generating that core. Our central home, Mickleton House, is right in the middle of a Cotswold village with a population of 1,500 or more. Some of us live in our own homes, up to eight miles away. We work in a wide variety of jobs in the neighbourhood – including some employed in Mickleton House to serve the community. We ask that visitors make a donation and anyone planning to visit should let us know in advance. We are not usually able to offer "keep in exchange for work". People who eventually make their home here normally do so after quite a long period of friendship and association with what we stand for. If you feel drawn to our approach please write to us giving some detail about yourself. In particular, you should say what it is that attracts you.

MICKLETON EMISSARY COMMUNITY

Status
existing community

Address
Mickleton House
Mickleton
CHIPPING CAMPDEN
Gloucestershire
GL55 6RX

Telephone
01386 438251

Fax
01386 438727

Electronic Mail
mickleton@
emissary.demon.co.uk

Number of over 18s
30

Number of under 18s
6

Year started
1980

Situation
village

Legal structure
registered charity

Open to new members?
yes

MONIMAIL TOWER

Monimail Tower is the only remains of Cardinal Beaton's Palace built in the 16th century. In 1985 a community was started on the land around the Tower. Most of the land is woodland. There is also a large orchard and walled garden. We now live in our first permanent building as well as some temporary huts. We try to share as much as possible from food and work to skills and resources. We eat a mostly vegetarian diet, organic if possible. The main areas of responsibility are the garden, the woods, building, maintenance and administration. We pay rent to the project and do not share incomes. We would like to find more ways to become self-supporting. We also like to meet people, play music, dance and generally have fun. We have meetings once a week and make our decisions by consensus. Our aim is to build a resource for ourselves and other people with which to learn how to live together in a way that is beneficial to all. We are open to people from whatever background to visit and take part. For more information please write enclosing a stamped addressed envelope.

Status
existing community

Address
Letham
CUPAR
Fife
KY15 7RJ

Telephone

Number of over 18s
8

Number of under 18s
1

Year started
1985

Situation
rural

Legal structure
registered charity

Open to new members?
yes

Monkton Wyld Court is a holistic educational workshop centre and registered charity run by a group of 16 adults and 7 children. The setting is a neo gothic Victorian rectory and outbuildings placed in a beautiful Dorset valley three miles from the sea at Lyme Regis. There are 11 acres of grounds which comprise a small farm providing milk, eggs, cheese and yoghurt, a one acre walled organic vegetable garden, lawns, childrens play area, woods and stream. The house sleeps up to 35 guests and includes two large group rooms, piano room, library, meditation hut, massage and healing room, pottery and arts and craft facilities. We also run a kindergarten and toddler group. Our structure is based in consensus but with leanings towards management, and our income is generated through a full program of courses and venues running all year round. We entertain up to 2000 guests a year which provides the business income and our pocket money. We are always open to short-term volunteers, and WWOOFers and occasionally are open to new residents. Please contact us for more information.

MONKTON WYLD COURT

Status
existing community

Address
Monkton Wyld
Charmouth
BRIDPORT
Dorset
DT6 6DQ

Telephone
01297 560342

Fax
01297 560395

Electronic mail
monktonwyldcourt@
btinternet.com

Number of over 18s
16

Number of under 18s
7

Year started
1982

Situation
rural

Ideological focus
sustainable living

Legal structure
registered charity

Open to new members?
yes

MORNINGTON GROVE COMMUNITY

We are a very mixed community of 14 living in two beautiful Victorian houses with a large garden, in a densely populated part of East London. We organise mainly through fortnightly meetings where consensus decisions are made. These are either "business meetings" (to discuss such issues as food, finances and repairs) or "get-togethers" (social meetings). Each household also has meetings to discuss the practicalities of day-to-day living. We have a unique rent system. We work out the community's expenditure and from this decide an average rent to cover costs. Each individual then decides how much they feel they can afford. If the total sum from everyone's rent is what we need *wonderful*, if not we enter into a process of negotiation. We have only once needed to do this. The ideological focus of the community is difficult to define. People are interested in ecology, therapy, the peace movement, films etc. We are gay and heterosexual and ages range from 25 to 52. There are also two lively young people of 15 and 18. Our "work" includes teaching, therapy, environmental organisations, nursing, and graphic design. We describe ourselves as a vegetarian, non-smoking community but some of us do eat meat and smoke elsewhere.

Status
existing community

Address
13-14 Mornington Grove
Bow
LONDON
E3 4NS

Telephone

Number of over 18s
12

Number of under 18s
2

Year started
1982

Situation
urban

Legal structure
industrial & provident society

Open to new members?
yes

The Neighbours is an ecumenical 'community of households' living in five adjacent terrace houses about a mile from the centre of Northampton. Each household lives separately and joins in communal activities, to a greater or lesser degree. One 'household' is a single person, another is a family of six. Apart from two retired, all the adults living in the five houses are working in 'ordinary' jobs, including a teacher, doctor, van driver, physiotherapist. We are trying to find a way of being together which is not too different from the way others live but which enables us to pray together daily and to support and encourage each other. The sort of community that can happen anywhere. There is a weekly community meal and meeting, breakfast together on Saturdays and open-house tea on Sundays. The large garden and some rooms are shared. We have a common fund for community expenses. Our statement of Purpose (revised February 1997) is '... to develop a community life which enables us to explore and share our faith and care for others according to the Gospel. Our wider aims are to encourage Christian unity and community and to seek understanding with those of other faiths.'

THE NEIGHBOURS

Status
existing community

Address
140-148 Ardington Rd
NORTHAMPTON
NN1 5LT

Telephone
01604 33918

Number of over 18s
7

Number of under 18s
4

Year started
1984

Situation
suburban

Ideological focus
christian

Legal structure
unincorporated

Open to new members?
yes

NEWBOLD HOUSE

NewBold House is a peaceful space to recharge your batteries, to spend some time surrounded by nature, to take part in a workshop or just to live in community, exploring creative ways of being and working together. We live in a magnificent large 100 year old house in seven acres of gardens and woodland. The emphasis in the garden is on education rather than self-sufficiency. Our diet is mostly vegetarian. It is possible to come and visit us for a few days or a week or two. Those who wish to experience community living in more depth can take part in a short term membership programme lasting three months. We have no set prices for being here and encourage guests to attune to their own contribution. We are part of the wider Findhorn community but independent of the Findhorn Foundation, becoming yet another expression of the same spirit. We welcome enquiries by letter or phone.

Status
existing community

Address
111 St Leonards Road
FORRES
Morayshire
IV36 0RE

Telephone
01309 672659

Number of over 18s
6

Number of under 18s

Year started
1979

Situation
rural

Ideological focus
spiritual

Legal structure
registered charity

Open to new members?
yes

We are a suburban community of 185 people, including 98 adults with special needs. We live and work together in 21 households, working on the land, and gift/coffee shop. We receive no salaries and our needs are met by the community. The management of the community is based on consensus with day-to-day decisions being made by mandate working groups. Our workforce is based on volunteers, with young people from Britain and abroad joining us (minimum age 19) for a minimum of one year. Our striving is based on anthroposophy, formulated by Rudolf Steiner. We work out of Christianity and celebrate the festivals of the year. Although we are members of a worldwide organisation, each place runs independantly, to meet the specific nature of that place.

NEWTON DEE CAMPHILL VILLAGE

Status
existing community

Address
Camphill Village Trust
Biddside
ABERDEEN
AB15 9DX

Telephone
01224 868376

Fax
01224 868701

Number of over 18s
158

Number of under 18s
30

Year started
1960

Situation
suburban

Ideological focus
anthroposophical

Legal structure
company limited by guarantee

Open to new members?
yes

OLD HALL COMMUNITY

Status
existing community

Address
East Bergholt
COLCHESTER
Essex
CO7 6TG

Telephone
01206 298045

Number of over 18s
40

Number of under 18s
20

Year started
1974

Situation
rural

Ideological focus
ecological

Legal structure
unincorporated

Open to new members?
yes

A one hundred and twenty roomed main building. Thirty five adult members. Nineteen children and teenagers. Seventeen guests. A dozen cows, two ponies, fifty chickens, thirteen geese, about forty sheep, three bee hives, several cats, no dogs and sixty five acres of fertile land. Two tractors and an assortment of fittings, three trailers, ten wheelbarrows, a dumper truck, two four wheeled trolleys. One hundred and fifty windows, twenty two toilets, twenty eight wash hand basins, thirteen baths, ten showers, twenty sinks and all the associated plumbing fittings and pipe runs. Miles of electrical wiring. Two acres of roof coverings, guttering, down pipes, sewerage runs, manholes, land drainage, fencing, ditches. All this and more needs maintaining. In a year we grow, harvest, store and grind three acres of wheat from which we make fifty loaves of bread a week. We grow and consume 1500 lb of onions, three tons of potatoes, a ton of carrots, a ton of leeks, wheelbarrows full of tomatoes, courgettes, marrows, sweetcorn, green beans and so on. We pick, cook, store, freeze masses of soft fruit, apples, pears, plumbs, gooseberries, strawberries, raspberries, loganberries and the like. From the cows milk is made butter, cheese & yoghurt. This food is used to prepare, serve and consume upwards of thirty thousand communal meals a year. Then there is the washing up, the cleaning, the scrubbing, the gathering, chopping and stacking of seventy tons of wood a year for the space heating around the building. We do all this because we enjoy it. It is not work but fun. Pushing a trolley down a supermarket isle picking cling film wrapped squeaky clean euro size sameness from the shelves is another life. Old Hall is a working example of Anarcho-Syndicalism. It has been for twenty one years now, though if you were to ask most members what Anarcho-Syndicalism was, they wouldn't have a clue.

Parsonage Farm is a community of nine adults and five children about 12 miles from Cambridge. We live in a large old house in three and a half acres of land at the edge of a large village. Most people have absorbing jobs outside the community so the main activity that brings us together is caring for the large organic vegetable garden that supplies most of our vegetarian diet (with occasional fish!). Every third weekend or so we work together with WWOOFers on the garden and we commit ourselves to one week a year of house maintenance. The community has a large Elizabethan barn where there is workshop space and the potential for development of other ideas. We eat together in the evening and support each other informally in childcare and life. The group is quite stable; the most recent member joined over four years ago and some members have been here over eighteen years. Some people here work in Delta T Devices, a co-operative business producing electronic research instruments. Delta T was formed by community members 20 years ago and is still going strong; employing 26 at the last count. We are a varied group with interests ranging from re-evaluation counselling to sea canoeing to African drumming and dancing. We like to relax together particularly in the summer when barbecues and trips to swim in the local brick pit (and cover ourselves in clay!) is a regular feature. At the moment we are full but may have places in the future. We encourage people who want to visit us to write and visit on a gardening weekend.

PARSONAGE FARM

Status
existing community

Address
128 Low Road
Burwell
CAMBRIDGE
CB5 0EJ

Telephone

Number of over 18s
9

Number of under 18s
5

Year started
1971

Situation
rural

Open to new members?
no

PATHFINDER FELLOWSHIP

Our purpose - Christian education for young people - Anglo-Catholic ethos - Community ecumenical - Monday Community night - weekly charge for accommodation to cover cost.

Status
existing community

Address
Bickersteth House
25 Sheffield Terrace
LONDON
W8 7NQ

Telephone
0171 727 5586

Number of over 18s
15

Number of under 18s
2

Year started
1922

Situation
urban

Ideological focus
christian

Legal structure
company limited by guarantee

Open to new members?
yes

We support a college for those with learning difficulties. Co-workers and their families live and work with 43 students. Our students have a range of abilities with mental, social, or emotional difficulties. Each of the four households are run on an extended family basis with shared mealtimes and common areas. Students live in the community during term time and attend classes or participate in the workshops and working life. The co-workers all work on a voluntary basis receiving no wage or salary but their daily needs are met by the community. There is always an international flavour to the community with usually half the co-workers coming from other countries. A small farm and vegetable gardens are worked biodynamically and provide much of the Community's needs. There are several craft workshops including a wood workshop pottery, weaving and basket workshop, with facilities for other crafts. A college building houses classrooms, a bakery and a hall in which plays, folk dancing, and festive occasions are celebrated. We are always open to enquiries, our usual request is that a potential co-worker has a year free of commitments and would be prepared to live, work and learn alongside others in the community.

PENNINE CAMPHILL COMMUNITY

Status
existing community

Address
Boyne Hill
Chapelthorpe
WAKEFIELD
West Yorkshire
WF4 3JH

Telephone
01924 254054

Fax
01924 240257

Electronic mail
101675.414@
compuserve.com

Number of over 18s
55

Number of under 18s
20

Year started
1977

Situation
semi-rural

Ideological focus
anthroposophy

Legal structure
company limited by guarantee

Open to new members?
yes

World Wide Web *http://ourworld.compuserve.com/homepages/Steve_Hopewell*

PEOPLE IN COMMON

Status
existing community

Address
*Altham Corn Mill
Burnley Road
Althan
ACCRINGTON
Lancashire
BB5 5UP*

Telephone

Electronic mail
pic@gn.apc.org

Number of over 18s
7

Number of under 18s
3

Year started
1973

Situation
semi-rural

Ideological focus
eclectic

Legal structure
*industrial & provident
society*

Open to new members?
yes

People in Common Housing Co-operative was set up in 1974. We are now based in Altham Cornmill, a historic early industrial building situated on Burnley's urban/rural fringe, which we have renovated to provide accommodation and workshops. There are about four acres of land, including riverbank, on which we are developing kitchen, ornamental and wildlife aspects as well as varied playspaces. All gardening is organic.Some of us live in separate units, while sharing some group facilities. There is a vegetarian communal group, which is hoping to expand.People's employment includes community development, gardening, counselling, single parenting, teaching cookery to disabled people and library assistant. On site we have a co-operative business making oak beams and timber for the restoration of buildings, which involves some of us.We have a strong commitment to co-operation, equality and the left, global and ecological perspectives. Our enthusiasms include gardening, cycling, playing bridge, circle dancing, art, radical politics, computers and sustainable lifestyles.We are looking for more people to live here to help develop the projects we are working on. We would particularly welcome a woman with woodworking skills to work in the timber business or to set up a spin-off to it. There is also a possibility for a horticultural project on the field. If you are interested in visiting, please write to us with details about yourself.

Sue langdon / Johnathan Helvt

We are dedicated to the ideals of the Christian Gospel in the context of community living and open hospitality. The Community at any one time will comprise 5-7 community members (leadership role), plus children, 2-3 volunteers (3 to 12 months); 1-2 asylum seekers (3 to 6 months); 20-25 guests (1 month to several years), up to 6 visitors (1 day to 2 weeks) and up to 10 wayfarers (1-3 days). Many of the guests have experienced a crisis in their lives (eg mental breakdown, alcoholism, drug addiction, marital breakdown, abuse, homelessness, prison, drop out of school or college etc). Pilsdon provides a working therapeutic environment of communal living, manual work, creative opportunities (pottery, art, crafts, music etc) recreation, worship and pastoral care, to help re-build peoples lives, self-respect, confidence and faith.

Founded in 1958 by an Anglican priest and his wife - Percy and Gaynor Smith - the Community occupies an Elizabethan manor house and its outbuildings in a valley in West Dorset, 6 miles from the sea. We farm nine and a half acres with a large kitchen and flower garden. Our life is inspired by the monastic tradition adapted by the seventeenth century Community of Little Gidding involving families, children and single men and women. The worship and spirituality is Anglican and sacramental, but ecumenical in membership. Community members are Christian, but people of all faiths and races as well as those with no religious commitment are welcome. Membership, guests and visitor enquiries to the warden.

PILSDON COMMUNITY

Status
existing community

Address
Pilsdon Manor
BRIDPORT
Dorset
DT6 5NZ

Telephone
01308 868308

Number of over 18s
34

Number of under 18s
6

Year started
1958

Situation
very rural

Ideological focus
christian

Legal structure
registered charity

Open to new members?
yes

PLANTS FOR A FUTURE

P lants for a future was established in 1989 to research, grow and supply information on edible and other useful plants. We are expanding the project and most of us are moving to a new site to establish a vegan Eco-village

Housing 50 to 80 people, this will include ecologically sound dwellings, alternative technology, a course centre and craft workshops. The aim is to be a working example of a sustainable, vegan lifestyle, with plants providing for all our basic needs. We have a database of nearly 7000 useful plants which can be grown in this country, and currently grow about 1600 of them. We favour growing perennial crops in a forest garden system. No money or specialist skills are required to join, just enthusiasm and commitment. We are also looking for people to look after our present site after we move. You can contact us at this address even after we have moved (hopefully in Autumn 1997).

Status
existing community

Address
The Field
Penpol
LOSTWITHIEL
Cornwall
PL22 0NG

Telephone
01208 873554/872963

Number of over 18s
8

Number of under 18s
1

Year started
1989

Situation
rural

Ideological focus
green, vegan, anarchist

Legal structure
company limited by guarantee

Open to new members?
yes

World Wide Web *http://www.scs.leeds.ac.uk/pfaf*

We are a group of eight families who live together, in self-contained units in Postlip Hall, a large, beautiful, Jacobean manor house with fourteen acres of land in the Cotswolds, even miles north-east of Cheltenham. Each family owns the leasehold on its individual unit, we all own the free-hold communally. Some parts of the main Hall and outbuildings, the fourteenth century Tithe Barn and the grounds are shared. The upkeep of the grounds, which included gardens, lawns, woodland, grazing for animals and a two-acre, walled, organic vegetable garden, and maintenance work on the Hall and Barn takes up a lot of our time. We come close to being self-sufficient in vegetables which, with the invaluable aid of WWOOFers, are communally grown. Pigs, sheep, chickens, geese, ducks, rabbits, hamsters, cats and a Shetland pony are looked after by individuals or groups of members. Public events of all kinds are held in the Hall, Barn and grounds. The Cotswold Beer Festival is held here annually. From May to September the Barn and Hall are used for arts and craft exhibitions and sales, drama, concerts, weddings, parties, feasts, folk festivals and barn dances. Apart from the enjoyment, the events form a valuable source of income which helps to pay for the upkeep of the buildings and grounds which includes long-term restoration work on the listed Hall and Tithe Barn. Decisions are made at the monthly Housing Association meetings or in more informal discussions between members. We are a small community, but not a commune. Most of the adults earn our living outside Postlip, although we enjoy eating together two or three times a month, we live independent family lives. What draws us together is being with other people, joining in what the group decides to do for fun, profit or necessity, sharing our needs as and when necessary and just being at Postlip! You are welcome to visit but please arrange a convenient date with us first.

POSTLIP HALL

Status
existing community

Address
Winchcombe
CHELTENHAM
Gloucestershire
GL54 5AQ

Telephone
01242 603797

Fax
01242 602237

Number of over 18s
18

Number of under 18s
13

Year started
1970

Situation
rural

Ideological focus
none

Legal structure
unincorporated

Open to new members?
yes

QUAKER COMMUNITY (BAMFORD)

Status
existing community

Address
Water Lane
Bamford
HOPE VALLEY
Derbyshire
S33 0DA

Telephone

Number of over 18s
16

Number of under 18s
6

Year started
1988

Situation
rural

Ideological focus
quaker

Legal structure
industrial & provident society

Open to new members?
yes

The Community's aim is to enable people to grow together spiritually in a caring environment, living together with a sense of shared adventure. In this way we hope to create a warm and loving atmosphere, which we are glad to extend to others.

We look after ten acres of land: some of it is cultivated as organic vegetable gardens and forest garden; most of the rest is managed as a nature reserve.

The three families have self-contained accommodation; individuals have bedsits. There are communal rooms in the main house, including a kitchen/dining area where the whole Community eats Friday supper and Sunday lunch. We have wheelchair access to the ground floor.

There is opportunity for corporate worship twice daily; on Sundays we host the local Quaker meeting. The Community has no hierarchy, and decision-making at our weekly house meeting is based on the Quaker business method. Once a month we set aside time to share feelings and reflect on our life together.

Members have a variety of occupations within and outside the Community. We have a pottery, keep goats and provide respite care. Visitors are welcome at our working weekends – please write with a stamped addressed envelope.

Rainbow is a street of 24 terraced railway cottages in an old part of Milton Keynes. Renovated and set up as a management co-operative by Milton Keynes Development Corporation in 1977, the first residents were a mix of 'alternative types' and previous tenants. Under "right to buy" legislation we collectively bought the houses at a discount in 1992.

RAINBOW HOUSING CO-OPERATIVE

We have a community house with meeting room, laundrette, workshop and office; 1/3 acre of land with polytunnel, chickens and ducks, children's play area and open space.

We do not live communally; each individual or family has their own house. There is an occasional street meal. People here are white but with mixed ages, jobs, class and sexuality. Many young children means a lot of shared childcare.

The Co-op is run by monthly meetings open to all members. Sub-groups manage finances, maintenance, landscaping etc. A workday or party brings out the best in us as a community. Occasional 'reviews' consider longer-term issues or how we relate.

Vacancies are rare and new tenants are chosen according to their level of involvement as prospective tenants and whether existing members feel that they are suitable. People not already living in Milton Keynes stand very little chance.

Status
existing community

Address
9 Spencer Street
New Bradwell
MILTON KEYNES
MK13 0DW

Telephone
01908 670073

Number of over 18s
34

Number of under 18s
20

Year started
1977

Situation
urban

Legal structure
industrial & provident society

Open to new members?
yes

REDFIELD COMMUNITY

Status
existing community

Address
Buckingham Road
Winslow
BUCKINGHAM
MK18 3LZ

Telephone
01296 713661

Fax
01296 714983

Electronic mail
Redfield_Community@
compuserve.com

Number of over 18s
15

Number of under 18s
12

Year started
1978

Situation
rural

Ideological focus
sustainability

Legal structure
industrial & provident
society

Open to new members?
yes

In 1998 Redfield is celebrating 20 years as a community. We will be welcoming friends and past members to a series of events throughout the year. Those years have seen a growing commitment to communal living. We live as a single household; eat together every day; and share all the domestic tasks, maintenance of the building and work on the estate. Much of our food comes from the gardens (where both organic and permaculture techniques are used) and the animals we keep. The mature woods provide fuel and include forest garden areas and both hazel and ash coppice. Decision-making is by consensus of all the members at the weekly meetings where our various activities are co-ordinated. We also spend part of this time sharing personal news and feelings about issues within the group. One meeting every month has no agenda and is given over to exploring and celebrating different aspects of our life as a community. Current projects include restoration and conversion of the stables into six flats and assorted workshops, as well as expansion of the conference centre. The plans include radical energy-efficiency measures and green building techniques. We have recently completed several straw-bale buildings and a living willow structure. The Redfield Centre is a conference facility used by many outside groups as well as for the Community's own events. Other ways to visit us include regular open days and well attended "Living in Communities" weekends. Spending so much time together throws up lots of personal and collective challenges. Working through these can be both rewarding and inspiring. We all feel that what we get from this way of life is directly proportional to what we put into it.

World Wide Web *http://ourworld.compuserve.com/homepages/Redfield_Community*

The Salisbury Centre is a large Georgian house and organic garden near Arthur's Seat. Established in 1973 by Dr Winifred Rushforth, our aim is to raise awareness of physical, mental and spiritual healing through classes, workshops, talks and special events. We live communally in a self-contained flat with room for six residents. Our diet is vegetarian. We aim to develop self awareness whilst supporting one another's growth. We have weekly work meetings for consensus decision making and meet for personal sharings.

SALISBURY CENTRE

The co-operative provides part-time work for five residents and works with the Salisbury Trust to maintain the running of the Centre. The Co-op is responsible for the daily business and creates the yearly programme. We have three terms, covering a wide range of subjects from T'ai Chi to dream-work and meditation.

The centre consists of a spacious studio, library, kitchen, meditation and healing rooms. Outside we have a lawned flower garden and vegetable garden surrounded by trees. A much needed haven for all in the midst of the city. We have been experimenting with sacred geometry, permaculture and regularly have tipi sessions and sweatlodges.

If you would like more information or wish to receive a programme please send us an A5 stamped addressed envelope. Visitors are welcome on a donation basis - prior booking essential.

Status
existing community

Address
2 Salisbury Road
EDINBURGH
EH16 5AB

Telephone
0131 667 5438

Electronic mail
trine@ednet.co.uk

Number of over 18s
5

Number of under 18s
0

Year started
1973

Situation
urban

Ideological focus
holistic/healing

Legal structure
company limited by guarantee

Open to new members?
yes

World Wide Web *http://www.ednet.co.uk/~trine*

SHRUB FAMILY

Status
existing community

Address
Shrub Farm Cottages
Larling
East Harling
NORWICH
NR16 2QT

Telephone
01953 717844

Number of over 18s
3

Number of under 18s
2

Year started
1969

Situation
rural

Ideological focus
ecological

Legal structure
company limited by
guarantee

Open to new members?
yes

Our communal name and address is misleading. We are not a farm, don't live in a cottage and if the 'family' brings images of Californian style cults ... we're not a family! We are a practical, secular, dirty-handed, music-playing, screaming kids community. Individual interests range from midwifery and politics to fine arts and drugs legislation. We don't have any particular communal ideal although we follow a pragmatic quest for sustainability and the hope of, one day, developing low-cost, eco-friendly, self-build housing.

We share a rambling 17th century farmhouse with room for a maximum of ten to twelve members. We are too small to accommodate communal businesses and most members earn their livings in conventional jobs. Although we are surrounded by beautiful countryside we are close to a busy road and motor-racing circuit. Combine this with the presence of two 18 year oldish members and you will see that Shrub is clearly not a place for those seeking a life of quiet spiritual contemplation!

Our mainly organic garden and polytunnel give us an increasing level of self-sufficiency in vegetables. Planting trees, large flower beds and herbs is a passion. We share communal costs and dedicate a day's work a week to the house and grounds. We welcome vistors, who should write giving a phone number. We are actively seeking new members both for the long and short term.

Simon is a community of rough sleepers and volunteers living and working together to care and campaign for street homeless people. We work for those who sleep rough as a way of life, those who are unable to accept existing help or for whom no adequate provision exists. We run a night shelter, residential houses of hospitality and a farm project. We also do extensive outreach work in order to make contact and build relationships with people living on the streets. We live and work in groups. Workers and residents share responsibility for decision-making and day-to-day running of the projects. We hold regular community meetings and daily breakfast meetings in each house. These meetings provide a forum for discussion and group support. The Simon Community needs both full and part time volunteers. No previous experience is necessary, but humour, patience, tolerance and the ability to accept people for who they are will be essential qualities for adjusting to life in Simon. Workers must be at leat nineteen yearsold and have a stable place to return to when they leave Simon. Room and board and pocket money £25 per week are provided for full time volunteers.

SIMON COMMUNITY

Status
existing community

Address
PO Box 1187
LONDON
NW5 4HW

Telephone
0171 485 6639

Number of over 18s
40

Number of under 18s
0

Year started
1963

Situation
urban

Ideological focus
humanitarian

Legal structure
company limited by guarantee

Open to new members?
yes

COMMUNITY OF THE SISTERS OF THE CHURCH

Founded by Emily Ayckbowm in 1870, the Community of the Sisters of the Church is an international body of women within the Anglican Communion, living under the gospel values of poverty, chastity and obedience, desiring to be faithful to the traditions of the religious life while exploring new ways of expressing them and of living community life and ministry today. Our worship as a Community in the four-fold Divine Office and the Eucharist, together with our personal prayer, form the centre of our daily life. We experiment with liturgy and try to be inclusive both in language and imagery about God and humanity. Creative activities enable growth and wholeness for vital living. These include: candle-making, painting, pottery, card-making, music, gardening, cooking, writing,... Sisters are engaged in a variety of pastoral ministries within and beyond the institutional church. By our worship and life in community, we desire to be channels of the reconciling love and acceptance of Christ, to acknowledge the dignity of every person, and to enable others to encounter the living God whom we seek. Community Houses are located in Australia, Canada, England and the Solomon Islands.

Status
existing community

Address
St Michael's Convent
56 Ham Common
RICHMOND
Surrey
TW10 7JH

Telephone
0181 940 8711

Fax
0181 332 2927

Number of over 18s
17

Number of under 18s

Year started
1870

Situation
suburban

Ideological focus
christian

Legal structure
registered charity

Open to new members?
yes

We are a busy social community in Bethnal Green, east of central London, comprising of 16 individuals with a wide variety of interests and occupations, plus Sesame our cat. Our community house is large, full of character and provides us with individual rooms, two bathrooms, shower, laundry room, television lounge, two large kitchens and a roof garden. We eat vegetarian/vegan food and aim to eat communally each evening, house meetings occur twice a month and decision-making is by consensus - reflecting our Quaker origins.

SOMEFRIENDS COMMUNITY

Status	*existing community*
Address	*128 Bethnal Green Road* *LONDON* *E2 6DG*
Telephone	*0171 739 6824*
Number of over 18s	*16*
Number of under 18s	*0*
Year started	*1973*
Situation	*urban*
Ideological focus	*diverse*
Legal structure	*company limited by guarantee*
Open to new members?	*yes*

THE SPACE HOUSE

The Space House is a quality non-doctrinal community. Acknowledging the universal shift in energies the House offers the opportunity to explore ideas and give "space" and time in a caring and supportive environment. The running of the house is shared with tasks such as cleaning, upkeep and cooking divided amongst the residents. Each person takes responsibility for offereing their energy and time to the development of the House. The Flame Foundation (a local charity) has its lending library here with over 1600 items on subjects such as counselling, spirituality, religions East and West, self-help, healing, alternative therapies and others. Once a week members meet, read and borrow items. We have a meeting room for two to twelve people with kitchen facilities. Current users include committee meetings, networking, meditation, individual practitioners. Other activities include "bring and share suppers", country rambles, "Stillness on Sundays", library activity days. We have a notice board with details of workshops, courses etc, both local and national. It is a focal point for this information to be distributed and discover for oneself what is going on.

Status
existing community

Address
8 Beaufort Road
SHEFFIELD
S10 2ST

Telephone
0114 267 0308

Number of over 18s
6

Number of under 18s
0

Year started
1994

Situation
urban

Ideological focus
non-doctrinal

Open to new members?
yes

Talamh is Gaelic for earth. We are 14 people who are fortunate enough to have 50 acres of organic earth. We also have a 17th century farmhouse, gardens, woodlands, a lake, working horses, musical instruments, a sauna, a growing fleet of bicycles and a lot of imagination. And a wall made of tyres. Talamh is adjacent to western Europe's largest open-cast coal mine, the M74, intensive dairy farming and a gravel quarry. As a housing co-op, Talamh promotes a responsible way of life, allowing individuals access to land and resources. It is idiosyncratic, active with a DIY style. To join Talamh requires organised regular visits followed by a two month trial period. Visitors are encouraged to visit Talamh at regular maintenance or gardening weeks, where they can work for food and board. We also request a small donation towards costs for those who can afford it. We also have room to take non-working, paying guests. Talamh is dynamic in its outlook and has plans for a charity, a visitor centre, and eco-village, wind turbines, and a worker co-op running courses on everything from self-build to shiatsu.

TALAMH

Status
existing community

Address
Birkhill House
COALBURN
Lanarkshire
ML11 0NJ

Telephone
01555 820400

Number of over 18s
12

Number of under 18s
2

Year started
1993

Situation
rural

Ideological focus
ecological

Legal structure
industrial & provident society

Open to new members?
yes

TARALOKA BUDDHIST RETREAT CENTRE FOR WOMEN

Status
existing community

Address
Cornhill Farm
Bettisfield
WHITCHURCH
Shropshire
SY13 2LD

Telephone
01948 710646

Electronic mail
100073.3502@c
ompuserve.com

Number of over 18s
9

Number of under 18s
0

Year started
1985

Situation
urban

Ideological focus
buddhist

Legal structure
registered charity

Open to new members?
no

Taraloka is both a community and a Buddhist retreat centre for women, to which women come from all over the world to experience the calm, beautiful atmosphere which has built up over the ten years of the centre's existence. The community exists to run the centre, each of its members playing a role in this. The community actively pursues the Buddhist way of life, following a daily programme of meditation, worship, work and communal meals. We also hold weekly business meetings and community meetings. Recently we have restructured our work situation by splitting into two teams, which meet daily to report in and to plan each day's work. We have an admin. team and a retreat organising team. We aim to be friendly and co-operative and decisions are arrived at through consensus. We are constituted as a charity. There is no entry fee, although new prospective members pay their own way for the three months of their trial period. If they are accepted as members they receive basic support. Celibacy is observed by all members on the premises but there is no bar to sexual relationships outside. As part of our ethical practice we are all vegetarians. Further information from our secretary.

Other Groups within the UK

We devise classifications systems to help you, the reader, find your way through a morass of material. But as fast as we invent new categories people seem to come up with new kinds of organisations that don't fit into any of them! So here's a bit of explanation.

Embryonic Communities
This seems a fairly clear category. These are groups that have an intention to form a community in the future and are at various stages in achieving this goal. Some are still at the individual pipedream stage and have not even had a first meeting of interested parties. Others, like "The Community Project" for instance, were on the point of exchanging contracts as we went to press. (In fact we thought that we'd have to invent a whole new category – "fledgling community" – just for them!) If you correspond with an embryonic group do not pester them for information on how things "will" be – they can only have aspirations and can not present you with actualities. Read this edition's "How to do it"

section (page 102) if you want to be fully aware of just how difficult it can be to set up a new community.

Multi-site Community
We've invented this category because we were getting an increasing number of groups that lived communally on several sites and just didn't fit into the standard pigeonhole of a community. However, our classification system isn't perfect and there are groups within the main UK directory that could just as easily come under this heading.

Networks/Support Organisations
There is obviously a sort of spectrum here. Some of these groups will exist to link up member organisations; others will be at a distance and have some role in supporting communities. Some networks are local, some national and some might just as easily be thought of as Multi-site Communities. All-in-all, we've done our best and hope that groups find themselves within the most appropriate category for them.

AMADEA CO-HOUSING PROJECT

Status

embryonic community

Address

care of Diggers & Dreamers

Telephone

Situation

rural

Ideological focus

spiritual/ecological

We intend to form a community with a spiritual as well as an ecological focus, to embrace all age and income groups. We will probably form a company to own the property we buy - and then sell long leases on the individual units, (ensuring that there are some to rent as well). There will be a communal building with rooms large enough to enable us to have meals together at least once a day as well as to hold meetings, etc. There will also be shared guest accommodation, workspace of all kinds, library, laundry, etc. We hope to cater for about 20 residents of whom 30% - 50% may be over 60. We would be glad to hear from younger interested people. We are looking for building land or suitable property in Devon but are open to other parts of the South West.

THE COMMUNITY PROJECT

Status

embryonic community

Address

care of 72 Lowden Road
LONDON
SE24 0BH

Telephone

0171 737 4403

Fax

0171 326 4961

Situation

rural

Ideological focus

none

We have formed a company limited by guarantee and are hoping to purchase a large property with 20 acres of land near Lewes in East Sussex. We anticipate dividing the property into self-contained units with a communal space. The members would jointly manage the shared parts, ie grounds and communal space. The company would have the freehold and individual members would be leaseholders. We are also planning to have a few self-built Walter Segal houses on the site.

We are convinced that living in a community can enable us to achieve the apparent paradox of living more cheaply and to have a better quality of life. Jointly buying a large property gives access to a kind of housing and grounds otherwise available only to the very rich. At the same time, this way of living should help us to live more sustainably.

ECO-SPIRITUAL COMMUNITY & WHOLISTIC EDUCATION CENTRE

Status

embryonic community

Address

care of Rosehill, Silver Street
LYME REGIS, Dorset
DT7 3HR

Telephone

01297 442691

Electronic mail

i.am@lightnet.co.uk

Situation

rural

Ideological focus

eco-spiritual

We are a small pilot group of 6 to 10 persons, families and individuals forming an intentionally co-operative, co-owned, eco-spiritual community; currently seeking a farmhouse and about 20 acres of forest land in South Devon. We will have self-built eco-homes individually designed to suit the needs of each family or individual. Initially we intend to convert the farmhouse for use as centre for community run courses and wholistic holidays, with themes of woodcrafts, arts, eco-home building, permacultural design, music and cultural traditions of the world. The philosophic basis of our community will be mutual love and respect for each other and all life-forms. Participants are free to practise whatever spiritual discipline they like. Children and adults alike will share the joy and delights of creativity, mutually encouraging the ever-emergent wisdom of their souls. Our school is life, and life our greatest teacher!

ECO-VILLAGE DEVELOPMENT

Status

embryonic community

Address

care of Diggers & Dreamers

Telephone

Situation

rural

Ideological focus

sustainable

A larger scale human settlement (50 to 2,500 people) with a basis of sustainability; designed for self-reliance in water, electricity, food, fuel, and dealing with wastes. Individual dwellings leased/owned/rented with access to and use of collectively managed area of common land. Prices of dwellings, and plots (for self-building), on sliding scale to suit people with variable resources. Participation of future residents in design of site, dwellings and infrastructure is actively encouraged. Green businesses and non-monetary trading encouraged to earn livelihoods; with healthy self-reliance and choice in relationship to global economy, as opposed to a pathetic dependence. Aiming for economic viability without charity, state grants etc. The aim is to develop a sustainable context for community, spirituality etc to evolve within. This project is still being researched and is looking for people interested in getting involved at a later date.

GROBY PERMACULTURE HAMLET

Status

embryonic community

Address

Lawn Hill, 57 Markfield Road
Groby
LEICESTER
LE6 0FL

Telephone

0116 287 6728

Fax

0116 287 6728

Electronic mail

alisonc@foobar.co.uk

Situation

rural

Ideological focus

sustainability

I am setting up a permaculture community based around a 500 year old cottage in nearly 1/2 acre of established garden which already has vegetables, soft and tree fruit. The house is designed traditionally with thick stone walls and thatch but there are opportunities for water-saving, energy conservation, waste recycling etc. I wish to garden bio-intensively and share my knowledge of Permaculture with like-minded people. There are two rented properties, a cottage in process of being sold which needs considerable repair and an empty site which could become part of the community. Personal growth and mutual support are important. Excellent access to Leicester by bus, cycle etc. The large commuter village is ripe for LETS as well. I have facilities for desk-top publishing and weaving and a strong interest in herbal medicine.

THE HEALING HIVE

Status

embryonic community

Address

care of Diggers & Dreamers

Telephone

01235 528028

Fax

01235 520067

A highly-qualified therapist (TA) and a published international new age educationalist, both warmly invite others who are lightminded to establish a Centre for hosting community-centred activities. Thanks to guidance, Diane and Christopher (Gilmore) favour the Midlands or Home Counties. Founding partners would share the upkeep and grounds with, hopefully, running water and organically grown fruit and vegetables. DIY divinity without dogma may well be freely expressed. Or, at least, tacitly recognised as being the vitalising energy for grounding responsible goodwill, plus ideals which aspire towards agreed working practices. Workshop facilities, five plus bedrooms are desired so smaller hotels are possible. Also larger properties needing renovation. All offers and/or ideas, if feeling karmically comfortable, will be gratefully considered. Availability to networking with the use of public transport essential. We invite a happy mix of skills, interests and experiences on a non-sexist, racist or ageist basis for our holistic Healing Hive to really buzz.

HEART SING

Status
embryonic community

Address
care of 2 Seaview Terrace
Tydraw, Bonymaen
SWANSEA
SA1 7BD

Telephone

Situation
semi-rural

Ideological focus
eclectic

Community of one, open to joiners. Vegan (although not strictly so). Politically anarchic (let individuals find their own balance together. Economically in support of recycling without use of money: links with the Prometheus Project (15 miles away in Caerau) and Give and Take (in Clwyd). Focus = we all know the theory that we do everything better in community; think better, feel better, act better - with high motivation. Physically, morally, spiritually, emotionally and aesthetically we can achieve more than as many so-called 'individuals' surviving independently. In practice many communes have transient populations. Purpose = to build a happy, creative, empathetic mixed and open group who want to commit enough throughout whatever buffetting the world throws at us. Yearly communal affirmation for members to join or leave. Open-plan house overlooking field near Swansea - structurally sound, internal detail to be comnpleted - available as property to start from.

LIVING GREEN

Status
embryonic community

Address
care of 28 Pancras Road
LONDON
NW1 2TB

Telephone
0171 837 1661

Fax
0171 837 1661

Situation
rural

Ideological focus
spiritual

Our group has been working together for several years with the long-term aim of establishing an eco-village – probably in Scotland. However, we recognise that this will take time, and have, therefore, worked out a long-term plan for how we intend to achieve this. Our first stage has been to set up an education and community development centre in central London, where we are currently based. We are now ready to take our second step – to establish a residential centre in rural Norfolk. This will provide accommodation for around twelve adults plus children, and will focus on growing our own food organically, and educating our children as whole people. To provide an income for members we will also run educational programmes for visitors, and training courses for local young people, and plan to establish a community business. We welcome new members - particularly those who are experienced, and/or qualified in early years education or in organic horticulture. Parents interested in home education are also very welcome.

PROMETHEUS PROJECT COMMUNITY

Status
embryonic community

Address
care of 31 Caerau Road
Caerau
MAESTEG
Mid Glamorgan
CF34 0PB

Telephone
01656 739813

Electronic mail
Robert@propro.demon.co.uk

Ideological focus
ecological

The Prometheus Project Community is planning to its property in 1998 to finance a roadshow to promote its ideals. It will then be a mobile community until further notice. The majority of diggers and dreamers are too poor to change the world, therefore we are determined to take our message to the richer members of society. They won't come to us so we must go to them. The message is this: "You, the rich, keep too much of your money to yourself to the detriment of us all. The poor spend all their money as quickly as they get it, and this keeps the system going". If the rich will pay for the building of a sustainable future, they will get to enjoy it first, and the poor will get the job of building it. For the moment jobs are what the unemployed poor need. We won't get a sustainable system worldwide simply by setting up a few communes in the English countryside. Those communes need to take their message about sustainability to where it will do most good. This commune intends to do just that. If you want to join before we go on the road, please get in touch now.

SYMBIOSIS EARTH SANCTUARY

Status
embryonic community

Address
care of Diggers & Dreamers

Situation
rural

Ideological focus
Deep Ecology

Proposed radical 'experimental' pioneer settlement inspired by traditional earth-oriented cultures will investigate the viability of living in a minimally modified natural environment under conditions which minimise the risks of contamination, corruption, and colonisation by mainstream Western culture. It is believed that increased long-term exposure to the conditions which have shaped humankind over 'biological time' will lead to a life-enhancing shift in consciousness through a reduction in the kind of surrogate experiences which have arisen over 'cultural time'. Accommodation constructed from indigenous materials. Diet indigenous, with meals shared. Work regarded as the primary source of spiritual enrichment. Ultimate authority ceded to Gaia and the 'rule of nature', mediated through pioneer consensus tempered by communal 'elders'. Guiding principles: 'Reverence for Life', austerity, frugality, fraternity, Love. Some things you will *not* find: electrical apparatus, plumbing; automobiles, fossil fuels, mail, trade, political activism.

'Only the foolish try to change the world; the wise seek to change themselves'.   George Bernard Shaw

ZACCHAEUS COMMUNITY

Status
embryonic community

Address
care of Diggers & Dreamers

Telephone

Situation
urban

Ideological focus
christian

We are an embryonic Christian community seeking new members. Our aims are to support one another through friendship and prayer, and to serve the wider community of Croydon. We would like to buy a large house together to act as a base for offering hospitality and hosting groups. We expect to have a fairly simple, non-materialistic lifestyle. Currently we meet twice a week. Members of the community must be committed Christians from any church background (or none), of any age, single or married. If you would like to find out more, please contact us and we can arrange for you to meet us.

COMMON GROUND

Status
multi-site community

Address
24 South Road
Hockley
BIRMINGHAM
B18 5NB

Telephone
0121 551 1679

Fax
0121 515 3524

We are a group of housing and worker co-operative based in inner Birmingham. We are all involved in such activities as vegan and veggie outside catering (including festival catering), organic vegetable and wholefood distribution, organic veg. growing, computer serving, vehicle maintenance, house maintenance and home educating. We work closely together in order to maximise the potential for co-operation. We share resources, ie vehicles, office space and equipment and labour. Most workers are waged by the businesses (we are aiming to pay wages to all workers). Becoming a member means the chance to learn new skills, through full training in your chosen areas of work and training in co-operative skills such as consensus decision making, facilitating meetings and mediation. Shared childcare is available and support for home-educating children. We are members of Radical Routes.

COMMUNITIES OF L'ARCHE

Status
multi-site community

Address
10 Briggate
Silsden
KEIGHLEY
Yorkshire
BD20 9JT

Telephone
01535 656186

Fax
01535 656426

L'Arche Communities welcome people with learning disabilities from hospitals or home situations, helping them grow towards independence in ordinary family housing. Assistants give the friendship and support that are essential by fully sharing life with them on a one-to-one basis. Employment in a l'Arche workshop or garden scheme nearby gives people new skills and confidence. Centres in Canterbury, Inverness, Liverpool, Lambeth, Bognor Regis, Edinburgh, Brecon and Preston

CORANI HOUSING AND LAND CO-OP

Status

multi-site community

Address

12 Bartholomew Street
LEICESTER
LE2 1FA

Telephone

0116 254 5436

There are two adjoining Corani houses in Leicester where six to eight of us live collectively and which act as a centre for other SPIL network activities (see also the network entry for Some People in Leicester). Housing is flexible and need not be collective. There is another Leicester house and one in Stafford. Homes are mostly urban terraces at present. We work large and small allotments and we own one in Leicester which is becoming a forest garden. Capital is not essential to join but those who have it are asked to deposit some with Corani. Income pooling is expected of members and this grouping is spread equally between Leicester and the West Midlands – and includes non-Corani people. Two children have been co-parented for ten years since birth and attend school. Decision making is essentially pragmatic; by consensus where all are concerned and otherwise with sensitive autonomy. We welcome, by arrangement, visitors who will help out or participate whilst with us. We probably have one or two room spaces in Leicester and Stafford for new members. Alternatively, we have been known to accept people and their houses! Corani is a non-equity-sharing, fully mutual body IE commonwealth.

GIROSCOPE CO-OPERATIVE

Status

multi-site community

Address

46 Wellstead Street
HULL
HU3 3AQ

Telephone

01482 223376

Giroscope is not an intentional community. Giroscope is very informal. As a worker co-op with the intent of providing housing for people we feel our primary function is to provide housing rather than create an intentional community. Decision-making is based upon common sense and practical necessity, in line with the housing needs of our tenants. Giroscope is an equal opportunity employer. We are open to anyone regardless of sex, race or disability. In terms of childcare, many of our tenants are single parents and as we charge no deposits this helps people in such a situation. Work undertaken is basic house maintenance with particular attention paid to green building products and practices. Most of our tenants live in two-up-two-down houses as well as larger shared houses. We also have three flats and a shop. Legally we are classed as a company limited by guarantee with charitable aims. We welcome enquiries by post, by phone or in person – no strings attached. Giroscope is a friendly, non-elitist group whose aim is to provide cheap, safe, comfortable housing with security of tenure. We are always on the lookout for new members with building skills and enthusiasm.

LEE ABBEY HOUSEHOLD COMMUNITIES

Status

multi-site community

Address

care of Archdeacon's House
39 The Brackens
Clayton
NEWCASTLE-UNDER-LYME
ST5 4JL

Telephone

01782 663066

Fax

01782 711165

There are currently three Lee Abbey Household Communities which are part of the Lee Abbey Fellowship - with larger communities in Devon and London. The three households are in Birmingham, Bristol and Blackburn. Members are either in paid employment or work voluntarily in the local area. The community life is based on daily prayer, shared finances and eating together. Members seek to live out the Christian faith in daily living.

NEW CREATION CHRISTIAN COMMUNITY

Status

multi-site community

Address

New Creation Farmhouse
Nether Heyford
NORTHAMPTON
NN7 3LB

Telephone

01327 349991

Fax

01327 349997

Electronic mail

nccc@jesus.org.uk

The New Creation Christian Community consists of 60-plus community houses in various locations around England. Some are rural, others are in city areas. Most of the houses are in Central England, but there are a number further afield. The Community is a part of the Jesus Fellowship Church, well-known to many for its Jesus Army outreach activity. Theologically, we're reformed, evangelical and charismatic, and support all the historic Christian creeds and doctrines. Our all-things-in-common lifestyle is inspired by that adopted by the Christians in Jerusalem in the first days of the church. All of us have experienced the life-changing power of God through faith in Jesus, and we want to live out this new life in a way that shows the love and life of God. Our backgrounds vary; some are rough, others more 'respectable'. As long as you are in sympathy with our aims and willing to participate in our daily activities and worship, you're welcome to visit us for a short or a long stay. Our Central Offices will put you in touch with local Community households.

CO-HOUSING COMMUNITIES FOUNDATION

Status

network/support organisation

Address

care of Diggers & Dreamers

Telephone

Co-housing communities, pioneered in Denmark 25 years ago and now being adapted in other countries combine the independence of a private dwelling with the advantages of community living. Each household has a self-contained private residence (rented or privately owned) and also shares a range of common facilities with the other members of the co-housing group – such as a community kitchen and dining area, playroom, workshops, garden, guest rooms, office and laundry facilities. The Co-housing Communities Foundation set up in August 1997 intends to co-ordinate research and development of co-housing communities in Britain, produce a legal and financial model for schemes and act as a contact point for individuals and groups interested in co-housing.

CONFEDERATION OF CO-OPERATIVE HOUSING

Status

network/support organisation

Address

care of 15 Spencer Street
New Bradwell
MILTON KEYNES
MK13 0DW

Telephone

01908 314685

The Confederation of Co-operative Housing is an organisation which represents its members on a national basis at Government level, the APPG (All Party Political Group on Housing Co-operatives); on the UKCC (United Kingdom Co-operative Council) and any other areas that arise. Its members are federations of co-ops such as the North-East Links, the London Federation of Housing Co-ops. and individual co-ops. Help for members and other co-ops is freely given and an annual conference includes workshops that are informative and provide training.

DEMANDING HEART

Status

network/support organisation

Address

care of Diggers & Dreamers

Telephone

Demanding Heart is a network bringing together those who wish to extend their spiritual lives and who are interested in developing new forms of spiritual community.

We feel a connection with both the eastern and western spiritual traditions but not their institutions. There is no particular spiritual ideology beyond using basic personal responsibility as a starting point but we are interested in developing a spiritual vocabulary based on shared personal experience.

Demanding Heart is a response to the many people seeking to make a "next step" in a spiritual direction.

ECO-VILLAGE NETWORK FOR THE UK

Status

network/support organisation

Address

CREATE
'B' Bond Warehouse
Smeaton Road
BRISTOL
BS1 6XN

Telephone

Electronic mail

post@beet.demon.co.uk

EVNUK is designed to assist in the development of sustainable settlements. A database of eco-village projects, individuals wishing to live in them and useful organisations is being compiled. This database provides the basis for a 'matchmaking' service to bring together people, land and resources in sustainable settlement development projects. EVNUK intends to make this service available on the Internet, but also to provide a human interface (by post, phone and fax) for those without access to the Internet. EVNUK's newsletter is available on subscription. The sorts of settlements supported by EVNUK are various; such as village scale (population about 1,000); new build and retrofit in urban and rural areas; co-housing; 'low impact' (teepees, benders, etc); communes; eco-hamlets; etc.

NATIONAL ASSOCIATION OF CHRISTIAN COMMUNITIES AND NETWORKS

Status
network/support organisation

Address
Woodbrooke
1046 Bristol Road
Selly Oak
BIRMINGHAM
B29 6LJ

Telephone
0121 472 8079

The National Association of Christian Communities and Networks is an ecumenical organisation whose membership includes individuals, long-established religious orders, 'new' communities, groups formed around contemporary issues as well as groups from diocesan/district and parish/local settings. Members share a belief in the power of small groups to make our world a more human place and seek the renewal of society and the church in a host of different ways. Members give their energy and enthusiasm so that they form a network where help, support, advice, information and encouragement are available. They receive a regular magazine containing articles, comments and news and participate in an annual general assembly. We are a movement whose members seek to be a voice within the churches to ensure that the living reality of community and the transforming power of small Christian groups is recognised.

RADICAL ROUTES

Status
network/support organisation

Address
care of Catalyst Collective Ltd
PO Box 5
LOSTWITHIEL
Cornwall
PL22 0YT

Telephone
01726 815649

Electronic mail
green.line@gexpress.gn.apc.org

Radical Routes is a network of independent co-operatives working for social change. We are creating bases from which to resist and challenge dominant structures in society and aim to develop an alternative economy and way of living. Through close co-operation we are taking control over property and land, developing economic and educational ventures and community based projects, all with the aim of empowering people at grassroots level. Radical Routes co-ordinates and provides a focus for its member co-operatives. These groups determine Radical Routes policies and control its actions. It also raises money for co-operative development. To this end it operates an ethical investment scheme which raises large amounts of money from sympathetic organisations and like-minded individuals. This fund enables member co-operatives to borrow money they could not otherwise raise at rates well below commercial levels. In this way the network is consolidated and extended.

SOME PEOPLE IN LEICESTER

Status

network/support organisation

Address

care of
12 Bartholomew Street
LEICESTER
LE2 1FA

Telephone

0116 254 5436

Fax

0116 255 5727

We are a city based co-operative network with a variety of practical activities: co-operative work (electrical and building businesses; radical bookshop; LETS office; vehicle pool; shared childcare; organic gardening; permaculture; income pooling; co-operative housing; capital pooling. There is a smaller group of people (two at present but ideally three to five) intending a lifelong commitment to each other, based on sharing of emotional and financial resources. We feel it is vital that local groups do not exist in isolation but are involved in wider struggles and broader visions. Our aim is to change the world! We are active members of Radical Routes Secondary Co-op – a network of radical housing and worker co-ops. Some of us are also working for people power; overseas development; Nicaragua link group; UK direct democracy and regional autonomy; recovering our genuine histories and cultures. We welcome visitors by arrangement and are looking for more people to get involved.

Outside the UK

This listing represents a sample of intentional communities around the world. In the main we have listed only those communities who replied to our mailing in spring 1997, so you can be reasonably sure that the information is up-to-date, but you will see from the text that we have also listed communities that replied last time and are confirmed by a current source. We have made no attempt to cover North America. The most recent edition of **Communities Directory**, produced by the Federation of Intentional Communities in the States, lists 550 groups there, and has an international list which includes communities not listed below. See North America section. Other good sources of information on communities worldwide are scattered through the following pages. Our thanks go to them for their good research and co-operation. When planning to visit any of these groups, please remember that they are people's homes. Write to them first, and wait for them to invite you. It is a courtesy to include an International Reply Coupon. Telephone numbers include the usual international prefix. Any prefix needed from within the country is given in brackets.

Eurotopia Hauptstrasse 5, D-84494 Niedertaufkirchen, Germany.
℗ 0049 (0)8639 6133 FAX: same
Publish an up-to-date directory in German of communal groups in Europe (and some outside Europe), with longer listings than we are able to give. Very useful. Unfortunately we received the 97/98 directory too late to use it for our research. Please do not order copies from the above address, but from
Ökodorf-Buchversand, Dorfstrasse 4, D-29416 Groß Chüden, Germany.
℗ 0049 (0)3901 471227 FAX: 82942.
ISBN 3-00-001311-3. Sven of Umweltwerkstatt Verden suggests you ask the Eco-village Project Centre (see below, Hamburg) for the latest Kommuja-Verteiler which is the network of (about 30) political communities.

Global Eco-village Network
Secretariat, Skyumvej 101, DK-7752 Snedsted, Denmark. ℗ 0045 9793 6655
FAX: 9793 6677 E-MAIL: gen@gaia.org
WEB: http://www.gaia.org
The Global Eco-village Network (GEN) is

an evolving network of eco-village projects around the globe, brought together initially by the Gaia Trust. People interested in linking into GEN should contact their local regional office. For Europe, Africa and the Middle East contact

*EVEN (see Germany), for Oceania contact **Crystal Waters** (see Australia), and for the Americas contact **The Farm** (see North America). They have a booklet describing their communities, and plan to publish a lot of good information on the internet: we at Diggers & Dreamers hope to be a part of this.*

EUROPE

AUSTRIA

Mag. Friedrich Köstlinger A-3710 Frauendorf 76. *If you want to let your life be blessed by the LOVE which created this world, and you feel you should do this in a community in Austria, please contact the above address.*

Sonnenhof Ritterkamp 7, A-3911 Rappottenstein. ℂ 0043 (0)2828 264 *[1995:] Founded 1987; small international community. Making safe learning environment for the adventurous exploration of group consciousness, and using this group energy to serve others. Central theme is unconditional love, and guidance from the higher self. Ecological co-operative lifestyle. Have not replied this time, but are listed in eurotopia 97/98.*

BELGIUM

La Moisson Asbl «Le 210», Houmont 24, B-6680 Sainte-Ode. ℂ 0032 (0)61 266447 FAX: 267072 *Aim: to reinstate people with a social handicap. Lodging: Central Home (administration and reception) - accommodation for 18 persons; Outbuildings: "Shalom" (4 pers.); Farm (3 pers.); Bastogne: family house and studio (1); Senonchamps: lodging for large family; Jemelle: appartment house (3 families and 6 unattached persons). We offer as well: psycho-social and administrative help. Our fulfilment: forest work; cattle breeding; gardening; producing of organic fertiliser and flower worms (for fishing); timber work.*

Communauté de la Poudrière rue de la Poudrière 60, B-1000 Bruxelles. ℂ 0032 (0)2 512 9022 FAX: (0)2 512 3286 *110 adults and 17 children living in five centres in Belgium (Brussels, Anderlecht, Vilvoorde, Rummen & Péruwelz). Pluralist: open in principle to all*

philosophies and religions; accent is laid on living and working together. Begun in 1958.

De Regenboog Norbert Gillelaan 20, B-1070 Brussel. ℂ 0032 (0)2 520 6586 *Started 1974 elsewhere in Brussels; over the last few years have been 10-15 people: a small core group and several short and long term guests. We try to live as a real community, sharing many things in daily life in a spirit of non-violence and living simply. We are searching ways to live in real and practical solidarity with the poor and oppressed in the world.*

CZECH REPUBLIC

Jelínkovo Rudolf Zidek, Vraclav 87. *A small group of young people who prefer life on a farm. Renovating an old farm house in East Bohemia. Open to people who would like to help with gardening and building. Vegetarian food provided; no wages. Space for a tent or caravan. Open from May to end of September. Please write first.*

Ladronka Autonomie, POB 223, 111 21 Praha 1. *Best known Prague squat, at Tomanova 1, Praha 6 - Brevnov. Plans submitted for use of building as an Autonomous Social-Cultural Centre, but eviction notices served. City sold site to the firm "Santé" in January 1997, but Ladronka still there June 97. Not a classic squat: people living there have quite a strong feeling of community living, and despite all the troubles they remain together and working. Nowadays about twenty people live there permanently; every Wednesday from 16h-18h the info-shop is open. They request petitions, letters of solidarity and/or donations to mailing address given.*

DENMARK

NATIONAL

Danish Association for Sustainable Communities (Landsforenigen for Økosamfund (LØS)) Thomas Steen Seiersen - Secretariat, Egebjergvej 46, DK-8751 Gedved. ℂ 0045 7566 4111 FAX: 0045 7566 4121 E-MAIL: gen@gaia.org *[1995:] Founded in 1993 to represent, support, develop and inform on sustainable*

*communities. The association now con-
sists of 25 communities and about 100
individual members, with focuses ranging between ecological, social and
spiritual. The association assists in the
establishment of new communities, both
urban and rural. It also lobbies for better
financing for environmentally friendly
housing, and the removal of other barriers to community establishment.*
1997: Address change supplied by
Global Eco-village Network.

Danish Village Association (L.A.L.)
Nørvad 4, Nysum, DK-9610 Nørager.
℡ 0045 9856 9393 FAX: 0045 9856 9484
E-MAIL: barbar@pip.dknet.dk WEB:
http://www.geocities.com/CapitolHill/2880
*L.A.L. the Danish Village Association is
an organisation of communities, mainly
rural. We aim to remind politicians of
the dispersed part of the Danish population and legislate for them so their living
conditions may be improved. Members
of L.A.L. are themselves associations,
based on sharing a community rather
than particular interests.*

SJÆLLAND (ZEALAND, COPENHAGEN)

Christiania Fristad DK-1407
København K. *About 750 people on old
military land, a network of communal
living, crafts and culture. Started 1971.*
Have not replied to us, but they still
exist, and Svanholm have confirmed it.

Dragebjerggård Sonnerup, DK-3300
Frederiksværk. ℡ 0045 4212 4011
Rural community. Have not replied, but
Svanholm confirms their existence.

Ecological Village Society (ØLK)
Hågendrupvej 6, Torup, DK-3390
Hundested.
℡ 0045 4798 7026 FAX: 4792 4581
*[In 1995] 59 adults and 26 children in
four of five planned co-housing groups
designed as an eco-village of 13
hectares. Organic farming, renewable
energy (active/passive solar systems,
Finnish mass-stoves, 450kW windmill),
water treatment (five composting toilets), local jobs and integration,
campsite.* Have not replied this time, but
Svanholm confirms their existence.

Svanholm Svanholm Gods,
Svanholm Allé 2, DK-4050 Skibby.
℡ 0045 4756 6670 (office hours)
FAX: 4756 6607
E-MAIL: svanholm@dk-online.dk WEB:
http://www.gaia.org/los/svanholm/index.html
*A large income-sharing group, in house
groups; consensus decision-making;
organic farming. About 70 adults and 40
children on an approximately 1000 acre
big estate. Started 1978.*

Vesterbro Enghaveplads 11, 2 th,
DK-1670 København V.
℡ 0045 3131 3048 *Inner city urban ecology project.* Have not replied, but
Svanholm confirms their existence.

JYLLAND (JUTLAND)

Andelssamfundet i Hjortshøj
Gl. Kirkevej 42, DK-8530 Hjortshøj.
℡ 0045 8622 2124 FAX: 8622 7000
E-MAIL: ove@inforse.dk
WEB: http://www.gaia.org
and http://www.inforse.dk
*Suburban community with 70 adults
and children. When fully established,
the community will consist of about 500
people in an area large enough to support self-sufficiency. Co-operative
housing, organic farming, optional use
of communal kitchen, a building company specialising in environmentally
friendly construction. The AIH aims to
further the ideas and principles of
democracy and co-operational organisation. The structure is based on
principles of a "resident democracy".
The members are linked to one of the
clusters of dwellings. If any member's
life is affected by a decision-making
process, the member has a vote in that
process.*

Gaia Fjordvang Skyumvej 101,
DK-7752 Snedsted. ℡ 0045 4242 5511 or
0045 9793 6655 FAX: 9793 6677
*Rural co-housing and course centre ini-
tiative. Address of info-point LØS above.*
Have not replied, but Svanholm confirms their existence.

Munach Egebjergvej 46, DK-8751
Gedved. ℡ 0045 7566 5687
Spread-out spiritual community in small

town. Have not replied, but Svanholm confirms their existence.

Den Økologiske Jordbrugsskole Centralgården, DK-9440 Åbybro. ✆ 0045 9826 5088 FAX: 9825 5099 *Organic farming school.* Have not replied, but Svanholm confirms their existence.

Ottrupgård Ottrupgård 19, DK-9520 Skørping. ✆ 0045 9839 2919 *Co-operative village, started 1992. 22 private houses and a communal farmhouse on the edge of the biggest forest in Denmark, with lakes for swimming. Farmhouse has dining hall for 100 people; most people eat together on the first four days of the week. Shed house for badminton, basketball, table tennis, football and large parties. The lofts and barn provide unused space which allows all kinds of dreams to be fulfilled. Every third Sunday is joint working-day. Heating from central boiler, augmented by solar power. Extraordinarily active cinema / theatre in nearby Skørping. 1.6km to the railway station. 38 adults, 27 children.*

Torsted Vest Slarisdal 3c, DK-8700 Horsens. ✆ 0045 7563 0138 *Suburban city council project.* Have not replied, but Svanholm confirms their existence.

FINLAND

Cultural-Ecological Club of Vanhakaupunki c/o Eero Haapanen, Viides linja 7 C 59, 00530 Helsinki. ✆ 00358 (9)0 701 6002 E-MAIL: ehaapane@cc.helsinki.fl *Free-time community on wild island near the capital. We devote ourselves to ecological living and inventions: solar energy, sailing experiments, ice-boating, small-scale food production (gardening and fishing). Guests welcome to visit and stay, especially in summertime, but please contact us first.*

FRANCE

NATIONAL

Réseaux-Espérance 98 Boulevard des Rocs, F-86000 Poitiers. *Network for personal development and grassroots actions: publishes a newslet-*

ter every three months; organises quarterly meetings and a one week gathering every summer. Please note that they have not replied this time.

BRETAGNE 22 29 35 44 56

Communauté de la Poterie La Poterie, F-22980 Plélan-le-Petit. *8 adults, 21 children: five families in five houses. We all work outside. La Poterie is a little village in the countryside. We want to live together according to Christian values. We are not an "eco-village".*

The Rowan Trust c/o The British School, Slad Road, Stroud, Glos, GL5 2QG, England. ✆ 0044 (0)1452 812229 FAX: (0)1453 759211 *Developing an Eco-village in Brittany. Sustainable living workshops and working holidays. Eco-homes for sale or rent. No particular religious or political ideals. Up to 50 people. Integration with local village by joint venture café, bar and shop. Welcome people of all ages, countries and cultures.* Have not replied this time, but sent this entry on a reply card from our last edition.

POITOU-CHARENTES-VENDÉE 16 17 79 85 86

La Sepaye Maison d'Accueil, Chatenay, F-79150 Moutiers sous Argenton. ✆ 0033 (0)5 4965 9131 *Welcome and support for physically handicapped adults.* Have not replied this time, but are listed in *eurotopia 97/98.*

CHAMPAGNE-ALSACE-LORRAINE 08 10 51 52 54 55 57 67 68 88

Communauté de Bois-Gérard F-10130 Chessy-les-Prés. ✆ 0033 (0)3 2570 6709 *Commune in the Burgundy countryside of about 10 adults and 10 children, linked to the del Vasto Arche communities. Trying to live simply, with a spiritual base: share income from external work, marionnette shows, breadmaking and more. Welcomes families when they need space together. Consensus decision-making. Forgiveness and reconciliation guide conflict resolution. Offer warm welcome to all visitors; please just warn them of your arrival!*

Ecolonie Community / Association
Centre Ecologique International, Thietry,
F-88260 Hennezel.
© 0033 (0)3 2907 0027
(2907 0112 to visitors) FAX: 2907 0094
*4 residents, volunteers, 30 members.
Seeking simple, self-sufficient lifestyle
without waste of natural resources and
energy. Horticulture, vegetable garden,
renovation with natural materials; interested in alternative energy, running a
vegetarian guesthouse and a natural
campsite; courses and workshops over
the summer. Information weekends:
about every second weekend of the
month (please contact us).*

BOURGOGNE-FRANCHE-COMTÉ
21 25 39 58 70 71 89 90

Ferme Accueil Visargent, F-71330
Sens-sur-Seille. *Spirit of the Ark
Communities. 8 adults, 16 children: four
families living separately, while sharing
certain activities and services.
Possibility of pursuing a very diverse
agriculture, and an alternative way of
life in general. Visitors are invited to
share in the life and work of the farmhouse in return for food and bed. Have
set up an association called Le Sénevé to
further communal spirit; planning to
build a collective space.*

RHONE-ALPES 01 07 26 38 42 69 73 74

Communauté le Sappel Le Grand
Champ, F-69510 Soucieu-en-Jarrest.
© 0033 (0)4 7805 1608 *Objective: to
allow the most poor people to find their
place in the Catholic Church.*

AUVERGNE-LIMOUSIN 03 15 19 23 43 63 87

**CRISE (Collectif de Recherche, d'Innovation
Sociale et d'Expérimentation)** Ancien
presbytère, F-23340 Faux-la-Montagne.
*Formed 1981; 7 adults, 2 children, cur-
rently living in two houses in the village
(with a central house). Alternative living
and working. Since 1989 have run a
sawing and planing business called
Ambiance Bois. Planning to create a collective space which would be a living
space, a space for work - with a library
and open resource centre about alternatives, and a space for welcoming people*

*on courses or otherwise interested in
their projects. Hoping to help revitalise
the Plateau de Millevaches. Open to new
people and new ideas. They have not
replied this time, but this entry was sent
in after our last edition went to print.*

Energy World F-87360 Verneuil
Moustiers. © 0033 (0)5 5568 2530
FAX: (0)5 5560 1456 *International community based on the spiritual teachings
of Michael Barnett, who is often there.
Currently 70 adults, 10 children. Own
school. Well and natural sewage treatment plant. Some horticulture and
husbandry. Regular seminars and festivals, most open to all. Staying possible
throughout year: prices on request.*

AQUITAINE-PAYS BASQUE 24 33 40 47 64

Beau Champ F-24610 Montpeyroux.
© 0033 (0)5 5382 6998
FAX: 0033 (0)5 5740 6565
E-MAIL: johncant@in-net.inba.fr
*Beau Champ is a community that works
towards creating an ecologically sound
lifestyle. During the summer we accommodate guests sympathetic to our ideals
and looking for low-cost holidays. Our
facilities are simple, including many
"alternative technologies" such as reed-
beds, composting toilets and solar water
heating. The house is surrounded by
woods, creating a private and tranquil
space. Please write in advance to
arrange accommodation.*

Hameau de Boussac F-47130 Bazens.
*We are not a community in the 1968
sense. We are rather a village community as villages and hamlets were lived
fifty years ago. The woods, land, springs
are comon property and are collectively
used, but every family has its own house
with one-acre gardens in complete pri-
vacy. The castle, with plenty of rooms
and activities, is also common property
and used collectively. By summer 1997
planning to be able to lodge and provide organic food for our visitors at low
cost. Group emerged from Ruralis,
which promotes rural community living:
Ruralis, B.P. 23, F-47130 Port-Sainte-
Marie. Pierre Gevaert has produced a
book, L'Avenir sera rural.*

MIDI-PYRÉNÉES 09 12 31 32 46 65 81 82
Bazian F-32230 Louslitges.
℗ 0033 (0)5 6270 9513 FAX: 6270 9541
Loving-Living-Place Bazian, international community, but right now all Germans; 22 owners of 48 hectares. 6 adults and 3 children actually living on the property. Open to newcomers, up-to-the-minute tendency, growing fast. Living committed to truth, sharing in total honesty, love, self-awareness, consciousness growth. No schooling for the kids; instead preparing an environment where they play, live and learn in their own rhythm. Intending self-sufficiency, ecological. Housing mainly in trailers at this point. Vegetarian food, some only raw. NO DRUGS!
Le Cun du Larzac route de St-Martin, F-12100 Millau. ℗ 0033 (0)5 6560 6233 FAX: (0)5 6561 3326
10 adults, 9 children. Experiment for "living and working differently" with a non-violent perspective. Le Cun is also a conference centre fed by renewable energy (water, wind, sun, wood) and a centre for research and education on the analysis of conflicts and their transformation.
Mela (Mother Earth Land)
Domaine La Lix, F-32260 Tachoires.
℗ 0033 (0)5 6265 3504 FAX: 6265 3592
[1995:] 40 adults. New age, holistic, green, arts and crafts, gardening, farming, macrobiotic vegan food, free alternative school, various living groups, 150ha, visitor house, healing house, study house. Have not replied this time, but are listed in eurotopia 97/98.

LANGUEDOC-ROUSSILLON 11 30 34 48 66
La Borie Noble
Community of the Ark
F-34650 Roqueredonde.
℗ 0033 (0)4 6744 0989
The Ark Communities were founded 50 years ago, and La Borie Noble is the eldest one. Lanza del Vasto was founder; his books are available here, in French or English. Important: ecology, manual work, simplicity of life, no electricity, self-knowledge, non-violence, vegetarian food, Gandhian philosophy, daily prayer

and meditation and yoga, political actions.
Les Amis de la Douceur et de l'Harmonie El-Faïtg, F-66230
Serralongue. ℗ 0033 (0)4 6839 6256
5 adults and 2 children living 850m above sea level in the charm of the Pyrénées Orientales, with 21ha of garden and surrounding forest/mountainside, our community is vegan and spiritual. We have a vision of a harmonious, gentle world, where love reigns, and all beings live peacefully together. Programme of events.

PROVENCE-ALPES-COTE-D'AZUR
04 05 06 13 83 84
Longo Mai Grange Neuve, F-04300
Forcalquier. ℗ 0033 (0)4 9273 0598
FAX: (0)4 9273 1818 *Started in 1973, with 30 people settling on 300 hectares on an abandoned mountainside in Provence. Now has over 150 active members and runs Radio Zinzine, a 24 hour free radio station, a visitors' village and a music group. Co-operative living and working; Co-founded CEDRI (European committee for the defence of refugees and immigrants), FERL (the European Federation of Community Radios) and the European Civic Forum which seeks to develop links of friendship and co-operation between eastern and western Europe. Has established a farming co-op for refugees in Costa Rica. Now has five co-operatives in France: a wool spinning mill near Briançon and four farms, including one near St-Martin-de-Crau, east of Arles, called Mas de Granier: a community and organic vegetables co-op. There is a co-op in Switzerland and in Austria. A new co-operative farm was launched in 1995 in Mecklenburg (NE Germany), and various projects have been developed in Transcarpathia (Ukraine).*
La Planète F-83120 Ste-Maxime.
℗ 0033 (0)4 94 96 39 64 *Collaboration with nature and with our own nature. Help welcome for a positive contribution to the farm, goats and garden. 7 adults and 5 children living in wild nature. Aim at survival and common-sense use*

of land. *Awareness of respect towards vegetarian and organic principles, health (no smoking) and love.*

GERMANY

NATIONAL

Eco-Village European Network (EVEN)
Ginsterweg 5, D-31595 Steyerberg.
✆ 0049 (0)57649 3040 FAX: (0)57642 368
E-MAIL: even@lebensgarten.gaia.org
WEB: http://www.gaia.org
Founded 1994 to assist in the following areas: Supporting the development of sustainable human settlements; Assisting in the exchange of information amongst the settlements; Making information widely available about eco-village concepts and demonstration sites. Global Eco-village Network contact for Europe, Africa and the Middle East.

Silke Hagmaier Ecovillage Project Centre, Dorfstrasse 4, D-29416 Gross-Chüden. ✆ 0049 (0)39 01471227 *Contact for the German communities network.*

Ökodorf-Institut (Ecovillage Institute) Goethestraße 21, D-79650 Schopfheim/Black Forest.
✆ 0049 (0)76226 5302 FAX: same
Seminars and advice for people wishing to join or set up a community. In our archives are lots of addresses of communities which don't want to be registered in an address list. It's best to visit us in our community, Delphin (see Baden-Württemberg). Otherwise we will send you a questionnaire for long-distance consultation. Please enclose two international reply coupons from your post office. Mail order service for books about all aspects of community living. Great festival with communities and other interested people every summer.

BERLIN

Synanon Bernburgerstraße 10, D-10963 Berlin (Kreuzburg).
✆ 0049 (0)30250 0010
FAX: (0)30250 00173
[1995:] Self-help community, founded in 1971 by addicts for addicts. Open to every user who is prepared to quit their addiction. Open 24 hours, recommend stay of at least two years. 500 adults and

their children live communally in Berlin, Brandenburg and Hessen. Three rules: no drugs, alcohol or other addictive substances; no violence or threat thereof; no smoking. They run a removal and transport business, a printshop and a pottery in Berlin, and a pottery and biodynamic farming and gardening in Hessen. Have not replied this time, but are listed in eurotopia 97/98.

BRANDENBURG (REGION AROUND BERLIN)

ÖkoLea Hohensteiner Weg 3, D-15345 Klosterdorf. *19 adults and 11 children, sharing living and working space on a former dairy farm. Priorities are ecologically sound building, water and energy conservation, organic gardening and educational projects. Goals include growth toward consensus decision-making and communal finances, and integration in the surrounding community.*

ZEGG - Centre for Experimental Cultural Design Rosa Luxemburg Strasse 39, D-14806 Belzig.
✆ 0049 (0)33841 59510 FAX: 59512
E-MAIL: zeggpost@zegg.dinoco.de
ZEGG is an international meeting point for questions concerning a future worth living in the areas of environment, non-violence and survival skills, arts and philosophy. A focus point to start interesting networks. We develop new forms of life, where love is freed of jealousy and fear and we enter into the experiment of international community. We call it experiment, because the living together of women, men and children is an organic process that we continuously question and reshape. We are working for powerful models for peace between people, between men and women, and between human beings and nature. We have a big 15ha property surrounded by a bright forest. ZEGG was founded in 1991 and is 80 km south-west of Berlin. About 50 adults and 12 children live here now.

SACHSEN (DRESDEN)

Frohberg Schönnewitz 9, D-01665 Krögis b. Meissen.
✆ 0049 (0)35244 41803 FAX: 41804

[1995:] 6 adults, 2 children. Organic gardening, natural energy, landscape shaping. Undogmatic spiritual. Seminar house, soft tourism, workshops for wood, electricity and metal. Have not replied this time, but are listed in *eurotopia 97/98*.

Lebensgut Pommritz nr 1, D-02627 Pommritz. ✆ 0049 (0)35939 385
[1995:] Green, garden/farm, crafts, technology, creativity. 30 adults and 20 children aim for self-sufficiency on 100 hectares. Supported by the regional government. Have not replied this time, but are listed in *eurotopia 97/98*.

THÜRINGEN (ERFURT)

Arbeitskreis Denkmalpflege
Burg Lohra, D-99759 Großlohra.
✆ 0049 (0)36338 61849 FAX: 61893
Restoring old buildings.

MECKLENBURG-VORPOMMERN (ROSTOCK)

Czar Nekla the Second
Stich ins Grüne 19, D-17121 Zarnekla.
5 adults, 4 children. Ecology, self-sufficiency, gardening / farming. Our common vision: to make a green, blossoming land with free and conscious human beings, where love can grow. You can visit us at any time. Railway station Rakow (9km). Started 1992, hoping to grow to 20-30 members.

Feuerlandkommune Ausbau 13,
D-17495 Brüssow. ✆ 0049 (0)30693 2507
[1995:] 7 adults. Anarchical, crafts and agriculture, work therapy self-help groups. We are looking especially for women who want to live in our community. At least 20 people could live here! Have not replied this time, but are listed in *eurotopia 97/98*.

Dorfgemeinschaft Klein-Hundorf
Postfach 8, Dorfstraße 6, D-19205 Klein-Hundorf. ✆ 0049 (0)38861 2533
We are a community of 23 adults and 13 children. We've been here seven years. We make music, crafts, dancing, mediaeval markets, animal husbandry, agriculture, gardening, Permaculture. Visitors welcome if you contact us first. Possible to join in our work in various areas.

SCHLESWIG-HOLSTEIN (N OF HAMBURG)

Schöpferisches Zentrum OASE
Schaarweg 70, D-23730 Neustadt-Rettin.
The OASIS is a Spiritual Centre for the development of creative consciousness. We are 20 people in the inner circle. Most live around the Centre. Our Association for the Development of Creative Possibilities has 80 members. Our seminars: THE SOURCE OF CREATION IN YOURSELF are pilgrimages home to yourself. We don't promise you anything, the universal wisdom is in the middle of yourself.

Basisgemeinde Wulfshagenerhütten
Post Gettorf, D-24214 Wulfshagenerhütten.
✆ 0049 (0)4346 5044
Christian community. About 70 people, adults and children, live together trying to share their life and their property like the first Christians did. All visitors are integrated into their daily life. Shop for wooden toys and organic cultivation. Engaged in peace work and the anti-nuclear power movement; partnership with a community in San Salvador.

HAMBURG

Arche Volksdorf Farmsener
Landstraße 198, D-22359 Hamburg.
✆ 0049 (0)40603 2490
The Arche Volksdorf is a Christian community with 18 handicapped and non-handicapped people as members. People with a mental handicap are at the hub of the community. We want their gifts to become visible for us and in our society. It is possible to live with us for a year or more.

NIEDERSACHSEN (BREMEN, HANNOVER)

Ecovillage Project Centre
Dorfstraße 4, D-29416 Gross-Chüden.
✆ 0049 (0)3901 471227
FAX: (0)3901 82942
41 adults and 17 children living in different houses in four villages. The present situation is seen as an intermediate position. We are realising an ecological village for 300 people on a piece of land that we bought in spring 97. Activities: ecological building, ecovillage planning, community-building,

national and international networking, seminars, bookshop, gardening, carpentry, free school etc.

Lebensgarten Steyerberg
Ginsterweg 3, D-31595 Steyerberg.
℗ 0049 (0)5764 2370
E-MAIL: dkennedy@lebensgarten.gaia.org
[1995:] 85 adults, 45 children.Spiritual and ecological focus (Findhorn orientated); permaculture field/forest, bakery, healing centre, art and sound workshop, textile workshop, community-institute (advice for seeking and establishing communities). Founded 1985. Have not replied this time; part of Global Eco-village Network.

Lutter-Gruppe Auf der Burg, D-38729 Lutter am Barenberge. ℗ 0049 (0)5383 1884 FAX: (0)5383 8500 *We are 14 adults and 5 children, living together not in a "strong" but in a softy anarchic community, and not a collective. We have some work spaces however where we are working collectively. We have some more businesses: silk screening T-shirts with political slogans and pictures, and a pottery. We have been practising a typical chaos economy for 17 years. We have written a book called das Kommunebuch.*

PrinzHöfte Simmershauserstraße 1, D-27243 Prinzhöfte.
℗ 0049 (0)4244 644 FAX: (0)4244 8679
[1995:] Centre for Ecological Questions and Holistic Learning. We are 12-15 residents and a few more who don't live here, but regularly come to help. Our subjects are permaculture, architecture, alternative energy, Freinet-teaching. On those and other subjects we do seminars, and our rooms can also be rented by groups. Visitors are welcome, but please call in advance. Have not replied this time, but are listed in *eurotopia 97/98*.

Troubadour Märchenzentrum
Bretthorststraße 140, D-32602 Vlotho.
℗ 0049 (0)5733 10801 FAX: 18634
[1995:] 10 adults, 15 children. Specialise in healing with fairy-tales. Have not replied this time, but are listed in *eurotopia 97/98*.

Umweltwerkstatt Verden
Herrlichkeit 1, D-27283 Verden.
℗ 0049 (0)4231 81046 FAX: 81048
E-MAIL: uw-verden@link-goe.de
20 adults, four children. VERbunt is a network of political/cultural initiatives, housing and workers' co-ops in the small town Verden. Members include: two communes, several housing co-ops, our environmental resource centre, an alternative culture-club, a veg-box scheme, self-help therapy groups, a town magazine, a food co-op, several political initiatives,... A large barracks building is being converted to an environmental centre. We are open for new members.

NORDRHEIN-WESTFALEN
(COLOGNE, DORTMUND)

Mutter Erde Holperstraße 1, D-57537 Forst-Seifen.
℗ 0049 (0)2742 8251 FAX: same
9 adults, 11 children. Founded 1983, inspired by Paramahansa Yogananda, an inter-faith community of people seeking personal development, and aiming for truth, simplicity and love. Looking for the eternal in the transitory, the unity of creator and created and the fusion of people's material and spiritual selves. Several houses in and around Seifen in beautiful countryside.

HESSEN (FRANKFURT, KASSEL)

Kuhmune
Dorfstrasse 12, D-37318 Schönhagen.
℗ 0049 (0)36083 141081 *Cows, milking, cheese making, vegetables and vegetable seed-production, working with horses, 3 children and a few big people (3-10). Spirituality has a place, especially "co-operation with nature".*

Kommune Niederkaufungen
Kirchweg 1, D-34260 Kaufungen.
℗ 0049 (0)5605 80070 FAX: 800740
50 adults, 17 children. Building, carpentry, mechanics, seminar house, typographic / layout, kindergarten, architecture, leather clothes, catering, organic vegetables, food co-op. Socialist, income-sharing; consensus decisions; communal education, anti-hierarchy,

ecologically-sound products, collective
work structures and living groups.

Ökologisch-baubiologische Siedlung
Auf dem Heckenstück, D-35075
Gladenbach-Friebertshausen.
✆ 0049 (0)6462 5090
E-MAIL: fred.eckert@t-online.de
*Ecological settlement using ecological
and natural organic materials for house-
construction; we maintain a flower
purification plant for the sewage, meadows with traditional types of fruit trees,
ponds, etc. The inhabitants agree to
being a close social community of neighbours - but economically independent.
16 of 18 planned houses are built and
lived in. Good for families with young
children - 38 already there.*

Projektwerkstatt Ludwigstraße 11,
D-35447 Reiskirchen-Saasen.
✆ 0049 (0)6401 5651
*[1995:] 4 adults, one child. Planning
much bigger project, including various
environmental projects, such as a radio
station, a workshop for making newspa-
pers and a laboratory for testing water
quality. Green, politics, arts, gardening /
farming, solar energy.* Have not replied
this time, but are listed in *eurotopia 97/98*.

RHEINLAND-PFALZ (MAINZ, KOBLENZ)
**Lernwerkstatt für neue Lebens-und
Arbeitsformen** Brunnenstraße 1,
D-54570 Niederstadtfeld.
✆ 0049 (0)6596 1366 FAX: same
*10 adults, 4 children. Eco-spirituality,
feminism, therapy and creativity. We do
not live in one building but in individual
flats and houses in our village. We've a
common centre where we meet. We run
a conference centre.*

Ökologie-und-Technologie-Betriebe
Eduard-Mann-Straße 1-7, D-67280
Ebertsheim/Pfalz. ✆ 0049 (0)6359 3498
*[1995:] 25 adults and 18 children living
together on 50,000 m² of land in a former paper mill, with differing and
financially independent setups. There
are various individually run enterprises.*
Have not replied this time, but are listed
in *eurotopia 97/98*.

BADEN-WÜRTTEMBERG
(STUTTGART, BLACK FOREST)
Communitas Agnus Dei Kloster
Frauenberg, D-78351 Bodman-Ludwigshafen.
✆ 0049 (0)7773 5836 or 7490
FAX: (0)7773 5805 or 7490
*[1995:] 29 adults, 25 children. Founded
1980: three places in Germany and
Belgium; also starting a community in
Ecuador. We are trying to live a simple
and spiritual life in following Christ.
Prayer and sacramental life is the foundation of our various activities: farming
and gardening, different kinds of music,
working with pregnant women and damaged people. In Belgium we have a little
school: École Don Bosco. We are interested in working together for a "culture
of love".* Have not replied this time, but
are listed in *eurotopia 97/98*.

Doernach D-72218 Wildberg.
✆ 0049 (0)7054 7522 (Saturdays)
*[1995:] 8 adults. BioVersity - Nature
Workshop. We play basic and applied
R&D. One of our focuses is Biotecture
with green roofs, green façades, edible
habitat, edible communities. We plant a
thousand trees a year. Booklist on
request, including self-build book
Natürlich Bauen by Rudolf Doernach.
Visitors by appointment only please.*
Have not replied this time, but are listed
in *eurotopia 97/98*.

Dolphin Community Goethe Straße 21,
D-79650 Schopfheim/Black Forest.
✆ 0049 (0)7622 65302
*Founded 1995; 8 adults, 8 children.
Focuses: Spiritual: tolerant (Christ, Sri
Bala, Sai Baba and other); Ecological:
permaculture, regional contacts; Social:
children, old people, handicapped people. Culture: music, chanting; History:
learning from communities in the last
100 years worldwide. Networking.* See
Ökodorf-Institut at start of Germany listing.

Wassermannzentrum
Hengstberg, D-74417 Gschwend.
✆ 0049 (0)7184 92800 FAX: 928080
*We Wassermen and women number
about 25. We live in a scattered village
community. In the centre is the
Wassermannzentrum, a conference cen-*

tre with self-help, therapy and meditation courses. Our common goal is the inner growth of every individual; we are open and tolerant, want to be as aware as possible and to live ecologically.

BAYERN / BAVARIA

Connection Medien GmbH Hauptstraße 5, D-84494 Niedertaufkirchen. ℂ 0049 (0)8639 60090 FAX: (0)8639 1219 *[1995:] 14 adults, 6 children. Spirituality, therapy, green, politics. Publishers of Connection magazine, people centre. Have not replied this time, but are listed in eurotopia 97/98.*

Projekt Eulenspiegel Dorfstraße 25, D-88142 Wasserburg/Bodensee.

ℂ 0049 (0)8382 89056 (restaurant 887875) FAX: 89056 *We are a working and living community that started in 1952 on Sylt (near Danish border). The project in Wasserburg began in 1976. At present eight adults and two children, we run an ecologically orientated restaurant, a culture centre with talking circles, events and seminars. Connected with this we have a small guesthouse. In addition we publish a small political journal about social tripartition, conservation and new living forms:* Jedermensch, *founded in 1958. Our project developed from an anthroposophical orientation, and some of us hold to that, but we are fundamentally open to all people.*

Kalia - gemeinschaft für kreatives leben und therapie Schermannsweg 3, D-81249 München - Lochhausen.

ℂ 0049 (0)89 864 1144 FAX: 864 2805 E-MAIL: KaliaCom@compuserve.com *"The personal is the political is the spiritual." We are a group of women and men of different generations. Our common work is both a practice consultancy and educational work. It is based on a holistic and sex-specific view and includes ecology, spirituality, politics, music and craft groups.*

Likatien - Stamm Füssen Eins Magnusplatz 6, D-87629 Füssen.

ℂ 0049 (0)8362 38993 FAX: (0)8362 6418 E-MAIL: likatien@neuschwanstein.com *51 adults, 55 children. Green, politics,*

spiritual, arts & crafts, therapy, gardening, technology.

Schäfereigenossenschaft Finkhof St Ulrichstraße 1, D-88410 Arnach / Bad Wurzach. ℂ 0049 (0)7564 931730 *[1995:] Since 1979 with fluctuating membership, several work areas: sheep farming, wool mail-order business, office for environmental advice, and more. No spiritual ideology. Have not replied this time, but are listed in eurotopia 97/98.*

GREECE

Centre of Co-operative / Creative Arts care of Agiou Dimitriou 102, Evias, 174 56 Ano Kalamaki, Alimos, Athens.

ℂ 0030 1 98 22 892 *New creativity centre and community, within the context of a spiritual-cultural Renaissance. Four acres, 400m from sea, near Nafpaktos in western Greece. Persons of sensitivity and vision invited to help complete the two storey building and open theatre. The centre is to become a focal point for unity through diversity, peace, inter-cultural communication, the arts, fraternal living and alternative ventures for a new planetary society. Will be democratically run, with all active participants considered as co-creators. You are welcome to visit after corresponding. Financial support would be appreciated.*

Myrrinounda -
Centre for Harmonious Living Griva 23, Halandri, 152 33 Athens. ℂ 0030 68 18220 FAX: 93426 *Community with retreat and seminar centre just outside Athens. They did not reply this time, but are listed in eurotopia 97/98; we have altered this entry in its light.*

The New Humanity Centre 100 Eleonon Road, Akroyali Avias, 24100 Kalamata. ℂ 0030 721 58172 FAX: 721 58035 *The New Humanity Centre is a new world centre providing space for the creative activities of the following groups: 1. The One Humanity-Universal Alliance: a group working for a One New Humanity All-Including World - the Evhumanity World. 2. The Ensophion of Humanity and the Esoteric Library - serving both for a new educa-*

tion and self-enlightenment as well as for holding international conferences by new age groups. 3. Spiritual retreat and accommodation for our visiting guests. 4. The Evhumanity *Periodical - a quarterly publication in English. We welcome Light Networkers living and working in Greece who are willing to offer voluntary part-time help for expanding the World Service.*

Sarakiniko PO Box 12, 28300 Ithaka. *Founded in May 1979 by 200 people. For orientation was worked out a self-representation paper with socialistic and ecological aims. Situated on an island in middle west Greece. A large rocky place with many olive trees. During the 18 years that have passed, practice has modulated the mental structures. The spiritual aspect is also here, and a variety of philosophical opinions. Community life has become more subtle and not easy to understand. Gardening, animals, music, self-discovery, a two-monthly journal and soft tourism are in practice.*

Gyürüfü Alapítvány
Arany János u. 16, H-7935 Ibafa.
✆ 0036 73 354 334 FAX: same
E-MAIL: bela@gyurufu.zpok.hu (Borsos Bela)
20 adults, ecological village community: crafts, farming, gardening, technology, sustainable rural environmental planning. Part of the Global Eco-village Network.

Atlantis An Droichead Beo, Burtonport, Co. Donegal.
✆ 00353 (0)75 42030
E-MAIL: 100531.2077@compuserve.com
WEB: http://www.ourworld.compuserve.com/homepages/a_graf/CRAC1.htm
Atlantis is still alive and kicking both here in Ireland and in South America (see their entry). Here in Burtonport we still have our very large house and run a hostel and garden; in west Cork things are moving with our 55 foot sailing boat. We are non-smoking, vegetarian, non-religious, mainly into health, people, music, theatre and environmental work.

The main big change for us over the last two years is that we are now running a rainforest campaign. It is very successful and has grown larger than we imagined. People interested in any of our projects, please contact us. Our green newsletters are available by e-mail. Atlantis books and a video also available. German contact: Andreas Graf, Neuhagener Straße 28, D-12623 Berlin. For financial donations, please contact Steve Thompson, 111 Highcliffe Road, Sheffield S11 7LQ.

Tyaya People Bocare, Sneem, Co. Kerry. *Leaving the 20th century behind. Living with 123 acres of land undergoing transformation. Living and teaching Paradise Garden ... self-supporting radical ecotarian - vegan living food - wild food - no mod cons - money free - barefoot. Blueprinting for our neo-neolithic future. True harmony with our conscious Living Earth. Practical and very grounded. Exploring our full evolutionary potentials ... telempathy with all, teleportation, personal and planetary physical immortality - all to be found in the Garden! Visitors willing to work and learn welcome* WWOOF *style; minimum stay one month. We are also seeking permanent residents. Write sending an addressed envelope, an International Reply Paid Coupon, a biro and blank paper, or you will not get a reply! Or, you can write who you are, when you are coming, for how long and why. Then we don't need to reply.*

Comune di Bagnaia Podere Bagnaia, fraz. Ancaiano, I-53018 Sovicille (Siena).
✆ 0039 (0)577 311014 FAX: same
15 adults; income sharing organic farming community, founded in 1979. Raise animals, tend cereal crops, vegetable garden, vineyards, olive groves. Would welcome visitors, especially from other communities, to help on the farm, exchange experiences and hospitality. They know of the following communities in Italy (who we haven't contacted):
Associazione Europa, *care of Antonio Palma, Fermo Posta, I-72012 Francavilla, Fontana (BR),* ✆ *0039 (0)368 571128;*

Il Casale, care of *Ulisse and Sandra, Azienda Agricola, Pienza (Siena), © 0039 (0)578 755109; Elfi del Gran Burrone, Comunità Agricola, Loc. San Pellegrino, I-51020 Sambuca Pistoiese (PT).*

Fondazione Bhole Baba Casella Postale 138, I-72014 Cisternino (Brindisi). *The ashram is situated in south Italy, in Valle d'Itria, a marvellous and sacred place with houses-trulli made in stone, a very ancient architecture. The trees are olive, almond and fig, as in Palestine, the holy land. The life is simple and spiritual, karma yoga, repetition of the mantra* OM NAMAH SHIVAYA, *meditation in action. Our guru is Babaji, Hairakhan Baba. We have a permanent dhuni (Dhyana Yogi Dhuni) with a sacred fire and a temple as in Herakhan. Arati morning and evening. The ashram started in 1979, willed by Babaji Himself. They gave us addresses of three other Babaji ashrams in Italy (who we haven't contacted):* **Centro Spirituale di Pace Haidakhandi,** *Località Monte Gaudio, I-14020 Villa S. Secondo (AT);* **Jnana Ashram,** *Santa Maria di Paguialla, I-06026 Pietralunga (PG);* **Hairakhandi Love Center,** *Vocabolo Villarosa, Località Corniole, I-06026 Pietralunga (PG).*

Damanhur via Pramarzo 3, I-10080 Baldissero Canavese, Torino. © 0039 (0)124 512226 FAX: 512150 *[1995:] Born in 1975; today has over 400 inhabitants and over 15,000 supporters. Damanhur is an innovative way of living. Land and buildings spread out over the valley of Valchiusella. Oberto Airaudi is inspirator and guide. Life is conceived as a constant meditation. The research of a full awareness in each everyday activity creates a way of life in which every action aims at contacting the soul and at promoting collective spiritual growth. Art and aesthetic research are fundamental aspects for the growth of Damanhur's society, and play makes it possible to open up to new visions of reality and to overcome the attachment to the fruit of the action and to habits. Celebrate solstices and equinoxes, and annual day of contact with the dead. Underground Temple of Mankind. Guided visits to community offered if booked in advance.* They did not reply this time, but are listed in *eurotopia 97/98.*

Piaggia Villa Piaggia 21, I-05010 Montegabbione (Terni). © 0039 (0)763 87020 *[1995:] We are an anarchic humanitarian commune, living as ecologically as possible with the land. The community started in Lower Bavaria in 1975 and moved to Central Italy in 1982. There are twenty adults and fifteen adolescents and children living in three houses on 100 hectares of hillside land. There are openings for new members. Visitors are always welcomed, but should first write.* They did not reply this time, but are listed in *eurotopia 97/98* under their old name Utopiaggia.

Rainbow Eco Peace Village Italia Cheggio, I-28030 Viganella, Novara. © 0039 (0)324 56315 FAX: same *[1995:] 12 adults, 6 children. Have established community as an interim while planning the rainbow eco-village. Permaculture, spiritual, arts, technology, politics. Yoga centre. Peace and Eco-Institute. Focalizer for European Rainbow Gathering. Visitors and volunteers welcome. Solar energy projects. Looking for donations to help in rebuilding of village.* They did not reply this time, but are listed in *eurotopia 97/98.*

Upacchi - Villagio Ecologico care of Eva Lotz Pedra, Ecovillaggio Upacchi 51, I-52030 Anghiari (AR). © 0039 (0)575 788195 FAX: 749330 *Ancient formerly abandoned Tuscan village; half of the houses have been rebuilt ecologically. At present eight families living there, seven more to come. Focus: building biologically, organic agriculture; still open for new members. Building a network of Italian ecovillages.*

NETHERLANDS

Emmaus Haarzuilens Eikstraat 14, NL-3455 SJ Haarzuilens. © 0031 (0)30 677 1540 FAX: 677 5832 *A ragpickers community. They collect*

*used goods, sort and sell them. Profits
are spent on projects for the poor. The
community is involved in different activities with and for the homeless.
Members are expected to work full time
and receive board, lodging, pocket
money, and full insurance.*
De Hobbitstee van Zijlweg 3,
NL-8351 HW Wapserveen.
✆ 0031 (0)521 321324
*8 adults, 2 children. Founded 1969, the
oldest community in Holland. Rural, self-
supporting, income-sharing. Main focus:
ecology, non-violence, personal growth.*
Humaniversity Foundation
Dr Wiardi Beckmanlaan 4,
NL-1931 BW Egmond-aan-Zee.
✆ 0031 (0)72 5064114 FAX: 5061844
E-MAIL: humaniversity@netland.nl
WEB: http://www.humaniversity.nl
*The heart of the Humaniversity is a
Therapeutic Community with a multi-
symptomatic approach. People with
problems such as addiction, depression,
isolation, are in the same basic program
as "healthy neurotics", spiritual seekers,
growth and therapy students.
Humaniversity Therapy is based on an
ongoing process of interacting and
learning in the moment. University status
since October 1996. Founders: Denny
Yuson (Veeresh), Mariet Wijnen (Samadhi).*

NORWAY

Vidaråsen Landsby 3240 Andebu.
✆ 0047 33 44 41 00 FAX: 33 44 01 91
*[1995:] A Camphill Village Community;
about 150 people in 17 households. The
village was founded in 1966; has a biodynamic farm and garden and various
craft workshops.* They did not reply this
time, but are listed in *eurotopia 97/98.*

PORTUGAL

Tamera Centre for Human Ecology,
Monte do Cerro, Reliquias, P-7655 Colos.
✆ 00351 83 63306 FAX: 63374
E-MAIL: tamera@mail.telepac.pt
OR tamera@zegg.dinoco.de
*Project started Spring 1995, connected
with Zegg in Germany. Resource centre /
research settlement concentrating on
ecology, technology, architecture, healing, sexuality, nutrition, art, spirituality*

*and the building of well-functioning com-
munities. Currently a permanent team of
ten people, with many other participants.*

SPAIN

Colectividad los Arenalejos Lista de
Correos, E-29567 Alozaina, Málaga.
*Libertarian community: 6 adults, 4 chil-
dren. Ecological agriculture applied to
trees and orchard. Ceramic craft. Social
ecology. Especially interested in children: affectionate motherhood.
Autonomous health: "vital hygiene". We
don't accept drugs. Write before coming,
and you must wait for the reply. Health
and Anarchy.*

Argayall OMC Valle Gran Rey,
La Gomera, Islas Canarias.
✆ 0034 22 697008 FAX: same
*Meditations, holiday-place for guests,
sessions, therapy, rooms for seminars.*

Associación de Arte Elemental Calle
Merced 33, E-11391 Facinas (Cádiz).
✆ 0034 (9)56 236488 FAX: (9)56 687139
*(That is our postal address: find us on
the Cádiz-Málaga road, 72 km, near
Tarifa; look for sunflower sign). 10-12
adults. On a mountainside, close to
beaches. Permaculture project open to
public Sundays and July and August.
Solar and wind energy, compost toilets,
natural foods kitchen. Also summer art
gallery, craft workshops, plus music and
performance space. Planned extension
of eco-hand-crafted bungalows for rural
tourism. Visitors work 30 hours a week
and pay 500 pts daily. Two week trial
period. All welcome but some Spanish
makes life more fun.*

La Urralera Apdo de Correos 88,
E-21200 Aracena, Huelva, Andalucia.
*Planned community. Yoga centre.
Permaculture; ecological garden.*

Walden Community Apdo. 120,
E-28350 Ciempozuelos (Madrid).
*This community's reason to be is personal,
interpersonal and cultural develpment,
resulting in the building of an essentially
new culture; such fundamental cultural
change allows us to really get out of doing
patchwork. Critical to this aim is the application of scientific psychology, with an
integrative, yet neither mentalistic nor spir-*

itualistic approach, as well as having in ecology the basic criterion for all our behaviour. We have a basically vegan nutrition, and have a non-poitical, non-religious, non-dogmatic approach. We have shared income, and participate equally in all basic tasks, access to knowledge, and in decision-making through consensus. Our social structure is based on true friendship and not on family. In order to preserve our identity as a culture, our outer contacts are controlled ones. A potential member can only visit us once a deep mail communication has made clear that he/she can come to see this community as the crucial option for his/her life. We are now three members, living in a small town. We aim to move in the middle-term to a fairly preserved rural location.

SWEDEN

Almviks Gard S-15395 Jarna.
℡ 0046 8 55152050 FAX: 55152006
E-MAIL: janesvara.hks@com.bbt.se
30 adults, lots of children. Hare Krishna farm community. School for children. Beautiful landscape. Lakes. Animals. Greenhouses. Bakery. Sawmill. Fruit orchards. Guesthouse.

GOVINDAS
Fridhemsgatan 22, S-11240 Stockholm.
℡ 0046 8 6549002 FAX: 6508813
E-MAIL: manidhara.acbsp@com.bbt.se
20 adults, no children. Hare Krishna city preaching center. Award-winning vegetarian restaurant. Cooking courses. Lectures in Vedic philosophy. Mantra meditation. And great ice-cream!

ISKCON
Korsnäs Gard, S-14792 Grödinge.
℡ 0046 8 53025772 FAX: 53025062
E-MAIL: bmd@com.bbt.se
50 adults, some children, Hare Krishna community, SW of Tumba (approximately 30 km south of Stockholm), in an old manor surrounded by hills and lakes. Activities: Simple living, high thinking. Organic gardening. Vegetarian cooking. Publishing of old Vedic literatures in 41 languages. Multimedia design. Graphic design. Festivals.

Kursgården Lindsberg
Lindsberg 10, S-79191 Falun.

[1995:] A course-centre outside Falun in Sweden. It originates from and is inspired by environmental movements, peace movements and solidarity organizations. The course-centre is managed by a community (ten adults), who try to live by natural resources. We use renewable energy resources as firewood and solar energy. They did not reply this time, but are listed in eurotopia 97/98.

SoliCentrum Box 16, S-28072 Killeberg.
℡ 0046 (0)479 30580 or 30515
FAX: (0)479 30245 *A Linbu community - esoteric school. Humans seeking to practically apply esoteric wisdom into our daily life. Three informing meetings will be given to people who show interest. SoliCentrum Art & Handicraft; workshops for stonecutting, silversmith, wood, textile, ceramic, music; café open during summer. Welcome!*

Stiftelsen Stjärnsund
S-77071 Stjärnsund.
℡ 0046 (0)225 80001 or 80210
FAX: 80301
Findhorn-inspired community with fairly loose membership structure. Beautiful surroundings 200 km NW of Stockholm. Residential courses all the year, working guest programme. Families welcome, hectic during the summer!

SWITZERLAND

Communauté de Chambrelien
CH-2202 Chambrelien NE.
℡ 0041 (0)32 855 1319 FAX: 855 1718
E-MAIL: renaudsouche@bluewin.ch
Christian ecumenical community, about 30 people. Organic garden, woodstoves, cattle breeding. Work only part-time outside community; consensus decision-making; nonviolence in personal relationships and political actions; care for children with parental problems and people with psychological difficulties; simplicity of living. Inspired by Arche communities of Lanza del Vasto and the work of René Macair. Please write in French and enclose stamped addressed envelope if possible.

Kraftwerk 1
Postfach 406, CH-8026 Zürich.
[1995:] A village in the city of Zürich for

700 people. Experimental architecture meets ecology. Another offspring from bolo'bolo. Contact via the Paranoia City bookshop at the postbox address given. They did not reply this time, but are listed in *eurotopia 97/98.*

Monte Vuala CH-8881 Walenstadtberg. ℂ 0041 (0)81 735 1115 FAX: same number at night (22h-10h) *Women's community: green, spiritual, arts. Hosts women only holidays and courses. Working guests can join for a month or more (five hours working a day for free bed and eating); working guests for two hours a day get a reduction on the hotel price.*

Hofgemeinschaft Waldenstein CH-4229 Beinwil (SO). ℂ 0041 (0)61 791 9328 *[1995:] 'Love as a direction and answer for the Earth.' Holistic living alternatives as solutions to present and future problems! Our Holistic Culture Foundation and the Waldenstein village community aims to recognise, try out and rework these ideas. We have a life school of holistic culture and a community: ecovillage and settlement, family, cells for new living. Please write for more information.* They did not reply this time, but are listed as Netzwerk Lebensschule für Ganzheitliche Kultur/Gemeinschaft in *eurotopia 97/98.*

NORTH AMERICA

USA

Fellowship for Intentional Community Rt 1 Box 155, Rutledge, MO 63563. ℂ 001 816 883 5545 FAX: same E-MAIL: fic@ic.org WEB: www.ic.org *Contact point for enquiries about communities in North America. Publish Communities Directory. The latest edition features over 500 listings for communities in North America, as well as 70 elsewhere in the world. Costs $25. Please contact them to enquire about postage costs. You can also try* **Community Bookshelf,** *East Wind Community, Tecumseh, MO 65760.* ℂ 001 417 679 4682 E-MAIL: bookshlf@eastwind.org WEB: http://www.crl.com/~eastwind/bookshlf.html

The Farm 556 Farm Road, Summertown, TN 38483-0090. ℂ 001 615 964 4324 or 2519 FAX: 2200 E-MAIL: ecovillage@the.farm.org *Contact point for the Global Eco-village Network in North America.*

SOUTH AMERICA

COLOMBIA

Atlantis Postal address: Jenny James, Apartado Aéro 895, Neiva, Huila.

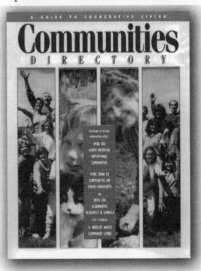

"To say that Atlantis in Caquetá is a farm on top of a mountain by a jungle is an understatement and undervalues what is in fact a wonder of human good intention, sheer hard physical work and ongoing tenacity." They run the Caquetá Rainforest Amazonia Campaign, and work in schools and with theatre. On the level of direct forest-saving, their next big aim is to buy some forested land several hours away in Chorreras. OK just to turn up. At Neiva bus terminal, facing the area where the buses come in, find the very last ticket office - COOTRANSHUILA - on your left (round a corner). Get a bus for Rovira, 4 hours from Neiva on the Guayabal road (not the Rovira in

Tolima). 3 hour uphill walk to their forest farm: ask for the "finca de los gringos(!)" Leave heavy luggage with Aminta at the blue restaurant with their huge sign outside, and they will collect it by mule later. In the Department of Tolima, they have another huge farm, where they lived for six years before coming to Caquetá, and which is still being run by members of the commune. See also the entry of their support house in Ireland.

La Atlántida - Fundacion Nueva Humanidad

Apartado 7566, Carrera 13 No. 8-44 Cali.
℗ 0057 92 885 3397
FAX: 92 513 1913
Rural Christian community. 20 bungalows; 200 acres. Members must grow own food. Zone is secure from violence, guerillas, etc. Prefer couples with or without children; singles only if equal number of males and females. No drugs, no free love; members must be very Christian. We believe Lord Maitreya is the Antichrist, Satan in a human body. Our goal is to reach perfection before actual humanity ends, between 1999 and 2000. Members wishing to get in are very well selected before entering.

NATIONAL

WWOOF Lionel Pollard, Mount Murrindal Co-op, Buchan, Victoria 3885.
WWOOF is Willing Workers on Organic Farms, and is co-ordinated by Lionel Pollard at the Mount Murrindal Co-op. Lionel is said (1997) to be compiling a communities directory. WWOOF can be an excellent way of visiting communities; UK address on page 223.

SOUTH AUSTRALIA

Cennednyss Community

P.O. Summertown, SA 5141.
℗ 0061 (0)8 8390 3166 FAX: 8390 1203
E-MAIL: dlg@adelaide.dialix.oz.au
12 adults, 8 children. Six houses and 15 acres in the Adelaide Hills. Started 1978; 15 km from GPO Adelaide.

QUEENSLAND

Crystal Waters Permaculture Village

1 Crystal Waters, MS 16, Maleny, Qld 4552.
℗ 0061 (0)7 5494 4620 FAX: 5494 9653
E-MAIL: cwcoop@ozemail.com.au
Intentional permaculture village, currently 100 adults, 55 children. A community designed for about 250 residents, established in its present form in 1988. 83 residential lots of around one acre, 500 acres of common land. Wide variety of dwellings and building styles: timber, pole-frame, brick, mud-brick, rammed earth. A co-operative exists to benefit its members financially and socially. Main operations are management of visitors' accommodation, community education centre, commercial kitchen and village centre. Bookings are essential for accommodation, tours and courses. Please don't just arrive and wander around. Oceania contact for the Global Eco-village Network.

West End Catholic Worker

269 Boundary Street, West End, Brisbane, QLD 4101. ℗ 0061 (0)7 38 441369
Small Christian community attempting to live out the basic Christian principles. Primary values are hospitality, resistance, common purse, and self-managed work.

NEW SOUTH WALES

Bundagen Co-operative Ltd

P.O. Box 82, Repton, NSW 2454.
℗ 0061 (0)66 53 4529
120 adults, 60 children. Rural, surrounded by National Park and State Forest. Permaculture, solar power, personal growth. Short-term visitors welcome.

Christians Box A678, Sydney Sth, NSW 1235.
E-MAIL: xian1@giga.net.au
We are approximately 20 adults in Australia and India, plus half a dozen kids. We live communally, share all possessions, and work for love, not money. Visitors are welcome as long as they participate in daily activities. In India (Tamil Nadu) work often involves menial chores such as cleaning toilets, but may include educational activities and first-aid clinic. In Australia we are always working on new ideas to raise public awareness about the long-term

effects of greed and religious hypocrisy. We have been inspired by Gandhian ideals and aim at practical applications of the teachings of Christ. We actively distribute literature expressing these ideals.
Koorool Community Candelo, NSW 2550.
© 0061 (0)64 932026 or 932019
Four families living on a mixed organic farm, on the edge of Tantawangalo National Park, also run a wholefoods shop in Bega. Visitors welcome on the basis of Willing Workers on Organic Farms. Please include a return postage coupon in your mail; replying to overseas mail gets a little expensive for us.
Yurt Farm - The Living & Learning Farm Graben Gullen Road, Goulburn, NSW 2580.
© 0061 (0)48 292114 (farm)
or (0)18 483960 (mobile)
FAX: (0)48 216999
475 hectare ex-sheep farm, now educational farm for young kids six to twelve years old. Families, cubs, girl guides, handicap groups stay in unique yurt village and learn about self-sufficiency (no television). 'Living with Less' includes milking cows, grinding wheat, bread and jam making. WWOOF members and overseas people always welcome.

AUSTRALIAN CAPITAL TERRITORY
Wyuna Community Inc. 24 Morant Circuit, Kambah, ACT 2902, Canberra.
© 0061 (0)6 296 2960 FAX: (0)6 231 3566
E-MAIL: mahatma@tpgi.com.au
We aim to live as an intentional family, to follow lifestyles chosen by ourselves rather than by circumstances. Our conscious intent is to realise this in a way which provides maximum opportunities for human & spiritual growth. We accept as our starting point the theoretical works of Dr Jim Cairns (ex-Deputy Prime Minister & Treasurer of Australia), whose energy was the catalyst for this project. Wyuna (which is Australian Aboriginal for "Clearwater") grows from the spirit of a very basic idea. We believe it to be the basic right of all life: "To be & do what one wants, so long as it does not intrude on anothers right." Focusing on ecologically sustainable technologies & energy sources whilst playing a pioneering role in the establishment of the Australian

community & co-operative housing sector in co-operation with our various Governments; we have created for ourselves a foundation of experience & skills which allows us to evolve into the next expression of Wyuna Community. We are happy to be able to share our fundraising knowledge Globally. "THINK GLOBALLY ACT LOCALLY."

VICTORIA
Commonground
PO Box 474, Seymour, VIC 3661.
© 0061 (0)57 938 257 FAX: 938 400
A small social change community that lives and works together from our beautiful bush property 95km north of Melbourne. Commonground's work focus is to support a broad range of community based organisations to operate effectively. To complement this, we operate two conference centres on our property. We use collaborate organisational practices and are best described as 'highly communal'. In 1997 we held the national gathering 'Celebrating Intentional Community'. Visitors welcome, preferably for two weeks plus and on a work exchange basis. Contact Kate Lewer or Ed McKinley.

Moora Moora PO Box 214, Healesville Vic 3777. *14 km outside of Healesville. Established rural community of 47 adults and 30 children in 20+ households on 230 hectares, mainly forest, with some mixed farm land. Membership shares available, options to build or to buy an existing house. Rural, alternative technology, earth building. Involved in WWOOF scheme.*

Ontos Health Retreat Gelantipy Road, Buchan P.O., Victoria 3885.
© 0061 (0)351 550 275 FAX: 550 277
We are 5 adults and 6 children on a 700 acre organic farm and health retreat, with a visiting population that has exceeded 200 for special events. Visitors welcome as part of the WWOOF program or health retreat guests. Property developed in 1980: yoga, meditation, bushwalking, organic orchards, huge gardens, excellent accommodation and food.

NEW ZEALAND / AOTEAROA
Centrepoint Community

PO Box 35, Albany.
✆ 0064 (0)9 415 9468 FAX: 415 8471
E-MAIL: cpoint@ihug.co.nz
*Founded in 1978, previously with 100
residents on a rural property of 93 acres,
going through some difficulties as of
1997, but hoping that something valuable will emerge from the process.*

Community Assistance Incorporated
51 Browns Road, Christchurch.
*Umbrella organisation set up 1970 for
the communes Chippenham, Mansfield
and Gricklegrass. Chippenham and
Mansfield are on adjoining properties in
Christchurch, and Gricklegrass is a 30
acre farm at Oxford, 50 km away.
Chippenham is currently a very child -
or teenager - orientated house, with kids
from four different families outnumber-
ing adults. Looking to build up their
adult population.*

Rainbow Valley Community
Box 108, McCallum's Road, Takaka,
Golden Bay. ✆ 0064 (0)3 5258209
*Non-income sharing; consensus deci-
sions; co-operate on different levels.
Focuses: children, farming, gardening,
arts and crafts, personal growth. Small
rural community of about 12 adults plus
children. Anti violence, drugs, alcoholism.*

Riverside Community
RD2 Upper Moutere, Nelson.
✆ 0064 (0)3 5267 805 FAX: (0)3 5267 037
*17 adults, 15 children. Pacifist / spiritu-
al, started 1941. Common economic
base, all assets held by Charitable Trust -
500 acres, dairy farm, orchards, forestry,
joinery. Consensus decision-making.
Two shared meals weekly. Hostel facilities available for visitors off-season. Book
about Riverside's history available.*

ASIA

INDIA

Atmasantulana Village
near MTDC Holiday Resort, Karla 410 405.
✆ 0091 (0)2114 82232 or 82291 FAX: 82203
*A holistic spiritual and healing communi-
ty based on Indian culture and Ayurveda.
We welcome all those who wish to stay
and participate in the community program, which includes yoga, meditation,
lectures and cultural events. We provide*
*healthy vegetarian food, and offer natural
Ayurvedic therapies for rejuvenation and
treatment of chronic diseases.*

Mitraniketan Community
Mitraniketan P.O., Vellanadu 695 543,
Trivandrum, Kerala.
✆ 0091 (0)472 882045, 882015 or
(0)471 451564 FAX: 0091 (0)472 882015
*150 adults and 300 children living in the
campus of the community. Training and
extension in Farming, various arts and
crafts, Transfer of Appropriate Rural
Technology, Experiment in Development
education, promotion of ecological and
environmental research and development, along with an exposure for
international living are major activities.
We aim to inculcate universal responsibility among people while working with
people at local and national level. Our
motive is a holistic approach to development. We are an education centred
community, started in 1956 by Mr K.
Viswanathan who is the founder Director.
He is a product of Tagore's Santiniketan
in West Bengal. This community is a non-
sectarian, and non-profit making one,
open to all irrespective of caste, colour,
religion and nationality.*

Osho Commune International
17 Koregaon Park, Pune 411001 MS.
✆ 0091 212 628562 FAX: 628566 or 624181
E-MAIL: cc.osho@oci.sprintrpg.ems.vsnl.net.in
WEB: http://www.osho.org
*Osho spirituality; meditation and per-
sonal growth. "The function of the
commune is to create an atmosphere of
encouragement - that you are not
alone." The beautiful 32 acre (13ha)
campus is open every day, and there is
no need to notify of your arrival in
advance. The Commune is not residential; long-term visitors often stay in a
hotel for the first few days, then find
accommodation nearby. NOTE: the
Commune does not have facilities for
children under twelve, or for people with
severe physical or mental problems, and
entry is conditional upon visitors testing
negative to HIV antibodies on arrival.
You can contact Pune Information
Centre, Osho Purnima Distribution,
Greenwise, Vange Park Road, Basildon,*

Essex SS16 5LA, England;
tel: 0044 (for UK) (0)1268 584141
E-MAIL: 101234.2145@compuserve.com

ISRAEL

International Communes Desk (ICD)
Yad Tabenkin Study Centre, Efal PO,
Ramat-Efal 52960.
FAX: 00972 66 753 603 (home)
Supplies information about kibbutzim in
Israel and up-to-date info about commu-
nities in 30 countries all round the
world. They publish the magazine Call,
with international communes news in
English. The kibbutz movement started
in 1909, and there are today 250 secular
and 17 religious groups.

AFRICA / MADAGASCAR
MADAGASCAR

Amour Sans Frontières
B.P. 55, 110-Antsirabe.
Convivial living community, seeking to
rediscover joie de vivre through work,
setting up various businesses for the
benefit of young unemployed
Malagasies, including penniless young
mothers abandoned by their families.
Currently three adults and two children,
and living with one of our parents, but
we are going to build our own house in
Antsirabe, on a hectare of land donated
generously by these parents. We're plan-
ning market gardening, tree-growing and
farming (permaculture if possible), for
the sustenance of the community and
visiting tourists. We've already started
an embroidery business, and we're hop-
ing to export and/or barter these. We
can also give embroidery lessons. In the
medium term we are hoping to create a
positively unusual international ecu-
menical village where young and old
can find what they're looking for. We
welcome letters of support and interest.

THE EDITORS

Sarah Bunker
Born 1964. Bunk is into
creativity, multimedia, compost
toilets, deserts and design.

Chris Coates
Born 1957. Cultural activist,
sometime engineer of the
imagination and rogue
carpenter/builder. Currently
having a mid-life adventure with
family and friends.

Jonathan How
Born 1953. Now living a post-
communal existence after 13
years at Redfield Community.
Full of wonder at the
convergence of technologies
which is taking place (in this pre-
Millennial phase) and all that it
makes possible.

Lee Jones
Born 1940. A founder member of
the Quaker Community at
Bamford. Having "retired" from
social work in her early 50s to do
an MA in Peace Studies at
Bradford University, she now co-
ordinates a community mediation
service in Sheffield.

William Morris
Born 1961. Lived for six years at
Lifespan and Ritherdon Road.
Compiles the overseas section of
D&D and produces his unusual
and wonderful Lunar Tree
Calendar every year. Loves the
bright, changeable moon and the
dance of the planets in the night
sky. Is an eccentric. Needs
money. E-MAIL:
williammorris@compuserve.com.

A good way of visiting communities is to join WWOOF – it's an organisation which helps people who run organic farms and smallholdings. Many communities are also WWOOF hosts.

Write to WWOOF care of 19 Bradford Road, Lewes, East Sussex BN7 1RB

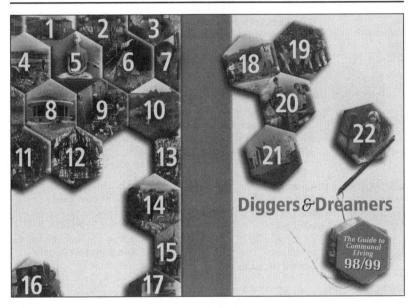

Diggers&Dreamers

The Guide to Communal Living
98/99

Cover design:
A patchwork of images supplied by many different communities,
sewn together by Jonathan How

1 Redfield Community, Buckinghamshire
2 "Tai Bwlch" – Graigian cottage near Mount Anelog
3 Aerial view of the Quaker Community, Bamford, Derbyshire
4 Horticulture at Chicken Shack, Gwynedd
5 Taraloka Buddhist Retreat for Women, Shropshire
6 Tipi at the Salisbury Centre, Edinburgh
7 A fulfiling life for people with learning disabilities at the Inverness l'Arche Community
8 New Humanity Centre, Greece
9 Ottrupgård, Denmark
10 Centrepoint, New Zealand
11 Bruderhof Community, Kent
12 The "Kama-Karzi" – Talamh's compost toilet, Lanarkshire
13 Osho Commune, India
14 A recent funeral at the Brotherhood Church, Yorkshire
15 Fondazione Bhole Baba, Italy
16 D&D editors meeting in the kitchen at Beech Hill, Devon
17 Grimstone Community, Devon
18 Laurieston Hall, Dumfries & Galloway
19 Community of the King of Love, Derbyshire
20 Open-air music at the Quaker Community, Bamford
21 Frankleigh House, Wiltshire – one of Britain's newest communities
22 "From small monkey-puzzles ...", Plants for a Future, Cornwall

Publications about holistic cultural change ... from the edge of time ...

Edge of Time is a marketing and distribution co-op which has grown out of Diggers & Dreamers. From books about communal living to lunar calendars and guides to ritual. Make cheques payable to "Edge of Time Ltd". Overseas orders add an extra £1.50 per title, please pay in £ sterling.

The directories may be out of date but these back numbers of D&D contain a wealth of interesting articles.

SPECIAL OFFER: BACK NUMBERS

Diggers & Dreamers 90/91   £2.50 post paid
ISBN 0 9514945 0 3   128 pp pb, b&w illus.

Diggers & Dreamers 92/93   £3.50 post paid
ISBN 0 9514945 1 1   216 pp pb, b&w illus.

Diggers & Dreamers 94/95   ~~SOLD OUT~~ t paid
ISBN 0 9514945 2 X   220 pp pb, b&w illus.

Diggers & Dreamers 96/97   £5.50 post paid
ISBN 0 9514945 3 8   224 pp pb, b&w illus.

The Commune
£10.00 post paid
Margaret Buckley
Chrysalis Press
ISBN 0 897765 00 2
386 pp softback
See review on page 34

Whiteway Colony
£15.50 post paid
Joy Thacker
ISBN 0 9521760 0 9
220 pp hardback, b&w photos
See panel on page 9

Places to BE 97/98
£8.00 post paid
Edited by Jonathan How
Coherent Visions
ISBN 0 9524396 1 1
160 pp pb, b&w illus.
Sister publication to D&D. A compendium of transformational holidays and places to "just be". Retreats, course centres and vegetarian B&Bs. Plus a comprehensive listing of venues for hire by workshop facilitators

Shared Visions, Shared Lives
£8.95 post paid
Bill Metcalf
Findhorn Press
ISBN 1 899171 01 0
192 pp pb, b&w photos
See review on page 75

catalogues from
BCM Edge
London
WCIN 3XX